Contents

Acknowledgements

We wish to express our heartfelt thanks to all those child welfare professionals, parents and children who contributed to this book.

Staying Together

Supporting families under the Children Act

MATTHEW COLTON
CHARLOTTE DRURY
MARGARET WILLIAMS

arena

362.828
COL.

© Matthew Colton, Charlotte Drury and Margaret Williams 1995

Published by
Arena
Ashgate Publishing Limited
Gower House
Croft Road
Aldershot
Hants GU11 3HR
England

Ashgate Publishing Company
Old Post Road
Brookfield
Vermont 05036
USA

British Library Cataloguing in Publication Data

Colton, Matthew
    Staying Together: Supporting Families Under
    the Children Act
    I. Title
    362.828

Library of Congress Catalog Card Number: 95-77821

ISBN 1 85742 265 1 (paperback)
ISBN 1 85742 264 3 (hardback)

Printed and Bound in Great Britain by
Hartnolls Limited, Bodmin, Cornwall.

1 Antecedents

Overview

Social welfare workers are universally committed to helping vulnerable families stay together whenever possible. In England and Wales, the idea that children are best brought up by their own families was given legislative expression in the Children Act 1989, which is widely seen as the most important child care law passed by the British Parliament for England and Wales this century.

This book offers an analysis of key issues in family support. It is informed by a major study on the heart of the Children Act: services for children in need and their families. The book embraces a unique range of perspectives, giving voice to the views of parents and children, social welfare practitioners, other professionals, and community and consumer groups.

We have consciously focused on issues that are of most interest and relevance to practitioners. To this end, we have attempted to write in a lucid style, primarily aimed at social welfare practitioners and students. The book includes considerable guidance on policy and practice as a contribution to the development of effective family support services. It can, therefore, serve as a source-book for those directly concerned with the welfare of children in need and their families.

In this opening chapter, we will set the scene for the remainder of the book by outlining the development of services for children in need. All the chapters which follow contain guidance that will help social welfare practitioners in seeking to develop effective family support services. The issues discussed in this book arise directly from a major empirical study on how social welfare practitioners and agencies are implementing Part III of the Children Act 1989. This entailed a study of the eight local authority social services departments in Wales to examine their objectives regarding children in need, policy and standards, targets and action plans. The progress of the Welsh departments with regard to implementing Part III of the Children Act was later compared with that made by eight similar Departments in England. Data on the other issues referred to were collected during an in-depth study of two Welsh social services departments. Interviews were carried out with some 103 social workers, 21 leaders of social work teams, 6 principal social services officers, and the lead child care managers from 16 local authorities. In addition, we talked with 122 parents and 123 children. Postal questionnaires were sent to a large number of voluntary child care agencies, community and consumer groups. Information was also gathered from key statutory agencies - for example, health, education, probation, and the police (further details of the study are given in Colton et al., 1995).

Chapter 2 concerns policies for helping children in need under the Children Act, and addresses key issues such the formulation of policy goals, the identification of 'children in need', and services for children with disabilities. Chapter 3 examines the part played by social workers in defining, identifying and prioritising children in need. Chapters 4 and 5 consider the views of parents and children. Do they feel that their needs are being properly met? Are they really consulted about decisions which have far-reaching effects on their lives?

Chapter 6 considers the role of other professionals: statutory and voluntary agencies, together with the contribution made by community and consumer groups. Chapter 7 looks at policies and practices in relation to the ethnic, linguistic and religious needs of vulnerable families. The concluding chapter ties together the material presented in a broader discussion of contextual issues which influence the activities of social welfare practitioners. Additional suggestions are made as to ways by which children in need and their families may be helped more effectively, thereby increasing their chances of staying together.

We begin this chapter by mapping the history of family support in England and Wales from the Victorian Poor Law to the Children Act 1989, embracing the post-war Children's Departments, the reform of the personal social services in the 1970s, and the permanence movement in child care. We then examine the Children Act: its immediate origins, aims and principles, and provisions for children in need.

The development of services for 'children in need'

The Children Act 1989 came into force in October 1991 and was heralded by the Lord Chancellor, Lord Mackay, as the 'most comprehensive and far reaching reform of child care law in living memory'. Moreover, the new concept of family support contained in the Act has been described as..."a quantum leap from the old restricted notions of 'prevention', to a more positive outreaching duty of support for children and families"...(Packman and Jordan, 1991, p.323).

Victorian poor law and philanthropy

The narrow conception of prevention replaced by the 1989 Act had its origins in the Victorian system of welfare. Holman (1988) has provided a valuable service by tracing the development of the concept of prevention. The Poor Law Amendment Act of 1834 was passed in order to establish a new regime which laid down that the able bodied would receive their keep only on condition of entering the workhouse. Conditions in these institutions were made as severe as possible, and included the separation of husbands and wives, the loss of voting powers (if those concerned had previously been enfranchised) and the compulsory undertaking of unpleasant and tedious tasks. The aim was to deter applications and compel people into seeking employment. Nevertheless, after 1834 the number of workhouse inmates rose rapidly, from 78,000 in 1838 to 306,000 in 1848 (Holman, 1988). The Poor Law became identified with cruelty and suffering. Some people quite literally preferred to starve rather than enter the workhouse, which was feared and hated by working class people until its abolition in the 1940s.

The failings of the poor law with regard to the care of children were observed by Dr. Barnardo, who identified two major problems of the state system: first, it depended on people approaching it while at the same time being designed to deter them from making applications; this resulted in hundreds of destitute children trying to survive on the streets. The second failing concerned the standard of care in the large barrack workhouses which stigmatised children, stripped them of their rights and individuality, and failed to prepare them for life outside the institution.

In response to such shortcomings, a host of voluntary child care agencies were established in the second half of the nineteenth century. These organisations, which were often initiated by individual philanthropists, attempted to provide for children's needs outside the workhouse system and sought to develop more humane alternative forms of care. Some of these societies are still operating today; for example: Barnardo's, the Rev. Thomas Bowman Stevenson's National Children's Home and Orphanage (now the National Children's Home), Edward Rudolf's Waif and Stray's Society (now the Children's Society), and Cardinal Vaughan's Roman Catholic Crusade of Rescue.

The voluntary societies varied in the emphasis which they placed on different methods of care (e.g., 'Cottage homes', foster care), but were identical in one fundamental respect: all conceived their task as that of rescuing children from bad environments and providing them with a fresh start. The idea of 'rescue' and 'fresh start' reached its logical conclusion in the practice of emigration. Between 1867 and 1906 Barnardo's sent 18,645 children abroad (Holman, 1988). By the close of the century, all the large child-care societies had followed suit. The

3

majority of children went to Canada; others went to Australia, New Zealand and South Africa. Most of the boys became farm labourers, while the majority of girls went into domestic service. Despite evidence of the unhappiness of many of the youngsters concerned, child emigration was practised well into the twentieth century and did not cease until after the second world war.

The voluntary societies partly saw their role as one of rescuing children from bad material conditions. To be sure, the social conditions of nineteenth-century, urban Britain were appalling by contemporary standards. However, the voluntary agencies also saw themselves as saving children from bad parents. This resulted in a punitive attitude towards those whom the charities considered to be irresponsible parents. Many of the children taken into charitable institutions were not, in fact, orphans. On the contrary, many had parents. But so far as the voluntaries were concerned, this was a hindrance. They were better off without parents.

Thus, although the Poor Law and the voluntary societies are often regarded as contrasting systems of child care, with the voluntaries formed in response to perceived shortcomings of the state system, neither was concerned with preventing children having to leave their homes or with rehabilitating children with their parents. Together, they established a pattern of child care that came to dominate child welfare policy and practice. First, both state and voluntary agencies combined to establish the principle that needy children were best brought up outside the influence of parents. Second, both linked stigma with the receipt of help. Third, the rehabilitation of children and their parents never became a policy within the Poor Law or the child-care societies. Fourth, the child welfare system was class related in that the children involved were mainly the children of the poor. Finally, any ideas of prevention were severely circumscribed.

The years 1900-39 saw little change in the Poor Law's attitude to natural parents. Once parents and children were placed in their respective institutions, the authorities saw no need or benefit from facilitating contact. Likewise, the idea of preventing children from entering institutions by supporting them in their own homes was not considered because it represented precisely what the Poor law was designed to eradicate; namely, 'out-relief'.

The post-war children's departments

However, the Children Act 1948 did mark something of a water-shed for services to needy children. The Act was based on the *Report of the Care of Children Committee*, better known as the Curtis Report; it transferred responsibility for the public care of deprived children to one central government department and one local authority committee - the Children's Committee, which

4

had a chief executive (the Children's Officer) who ran the newly created Children's Departments. This served to remove the confusions and inefficiencies associated with the previous system in which responsibilities had been fragmented between many departments. The 1948 Act also signified the end of the Poor Law's influence over children; it became law on the same day as the National Assistance Act which abolished the Poor Law.

Nevertheless, although the 1948 Act represented a more humane approach towards the care of deprived children, it did not directly promote practice geared to preventing children having to be received into public care. The Act did, however, put the concept of rehabilitation on the statute book. Further, the new personnel responsible for the Children's Departments - the Children's Officers and, their subordinates, the Child-care Officers - established professional associations that later pressed for powers to carry out preventive work with families.

The case for prevention was also partly aided by other social welfare legislation of the 1940s initiated by the Labour Government. In the first place, this helped to reduce extreme poverty, which in turn undermined the position of those who wanted to 'rescue' children from evil environments to which they should never return. Second, employment, decent housing conditions and improved health offered the basis of family life, and thus made attempts to prevent children from leaving their homes a more feasible objective.

The claims of Children's Officers that early intervention was vital to prevent reception into care were reinforced by concern about the high costs of residential care, the high rates of fostering breakdown and the theory, popularised by Bowlby (1952), that children's psychological health was impaired by separating them from their parents. Moreover, the Children and Young Persons (Amendment) Act 1952 placed a duty on Children's Departments to investigate any information suggesting that a child was in need of care and protection whether or not the neglect was 'wilful'.

Packman (1975) reports that by the mid-1950s, most Children's Departments were actively engaged in preventing the admission of children to care. Around this time, a second aspect of prevention, that of preventing delinquency, was receiving considerable attention. This culminated in the publication of the Ingleby Report in 1960 (*Report of the Committee on Children and Young Persons*, 1960), which was the first government report to give prominence to prevention. The Ingleby Report viewed offenses as symptoms of family problems which should, therefore, be treated by the courts in the context of the family. A number of its recommendations were given legislative expression, and were of significance for prevention. For example, Section 1 of the Children and Young Persons Act 1963 placed a duty on social workers to help any family whose children were not in the care of the local authority. This significantly extended the work of the Children's Departments from being a curative, rescue service to one with the virtually infinite brief of promoting the welfare of children by working with the family as a whole.

The 1960s were distinguished by a number of other government and party political reports on the role of prevention and the causes and treatment of delinquency. In England and Wales, this led to the Children and Young Persons Act 1969. This Act attempted to integrate the ways of dealing with deprived and delinquent youngsters, to reduce the role of criminal proceedings, and to place both the prevention and treatment of offenders mainly in the hands of local authority Children's Departments. Although the Act was never fully implemented, it did introduce significant changes, which included intermediate treatment; a service aimed at preventing youngsters from entering care through supervision and a range of community-based activities.

Reform of the personal social services

Throughout the 1960s, political party publications, government reports and independent bodies argued in favour of reforming the local authority personal social services. In December 1965, Sir Frederic Seebohm was appointed to chair a government committee to ...'consider what changes are desirable to secure an effective family service'...(*The Report of the Committee on Local Authority and Allied Social Services*, 1968). The Seebohm Report is a major landmark in the development of the social services. It recommended that the following separate services should be amalgamated into a single social services department: children's and welfare departments, educational welfare, child guidance, home-help, mental health, day nurseries and certain housing welfare services. The scope of the report was broad. A whole chapter was devoted to the prevention of social distress. The report wanted services to be accessible to communities: it wanted communities to participate in the running of services, and for services to be directed toward the well-being of the whole community and not only to social casualties. By contrast with the visionary nature of the Seebohm Report, the associated parliamentary Bill published in 1970 was a brief, technical document, which did little more than provide for the reorganisation of the social services along the lines proposed. The local Authority Social Services Act came into operation on 1 April 1971.

After an optimistic period of early growth, the newly created Social Services Departments (SSDs) were severely criticised for devoting insufficient attention to prevention and rehabilitation. The SSDs were also said to have lost the skill to place children with good quality substitute parents. Quite simply, many believed that reorganisation had led to a deterioration in the quality of children's services. This was attributed to the detrimental impact of the generic social worker, staff changes, pressure of work and the sheer size and complexity of the new Departments (Parker, 1980)

In addition to the reorganisation of the social services, the impact of rising poverty and deprivation also made it difficult for social workers to undertake prevention during the 1970s. Despite general improvements in the quality of life brought about by the social reforms of the post-war period, poverty did not disappear (Townsend, 1979). This meant greater demands on SSDs, who in effect became rationers of services. Social workers came to be seem more as withholders of resources than as distributors which served to undermine their standing in the eyes of those who they were seeking to help (NISW, 1982).

The permanency movement

Public perception of social work was also damaged by other events that occurred in the 1970s, and which resulted in renewed stress on removing children permanently from their natural parents. One such event was the horrific death of Maria Colwell, which precipitated a savage media assault on social workers, who were accused of worshipping the 'blood tie' between children and their natural parents (Parton, 1985). Another significant occurrence was the publication in 1973 of Rowe and Lambert's book, *Children Who Wait*, (Rowe and Lambert, 1973). The authors estimated that some 6,000 of their sample of children in care were allowed to 'drift' without decisions being made for their permanent futures. The book was unfairly used as ammunition by the growing adoption lobby. Maria Colwell's tragic death and Rowe and Lambert's research appeared to show that children were in danger from inadequate parents and that many could be placed with substitute parents.

Some argued that removal from such parents should be permanent (Goldstein, Freud and Solnit, 1973 and 1979). The 'cycle of deprivation' thesis, propagated by Sir Keith Joseph around the same time, also reinforced the doctrines of removal and permanence by stressing the inter-generational aspects of poor parenting and by identifying child abuse as being mainly a problem of the lower social classes.

The Children Bill 1975 reflected the ideas of the permanency movement. Part One of the Bill contained proposals to improve the coverage and practice of adoption agencies, and to reduce the powers of natural parents, in certain cases, to refuse consent to adoption orders. Part Two introduced the new order of custodianship, under which substitute parents, in certain circumstances, could gain legal custody over children outside adoption. Part Three gave local authorities increased powers to assume parental rights over children. Parton (1985) observes that the Bill attempted to give local authorities much greater control over the lives of children in their care, to allow an easier severance of parental links and give greater security to children in their substitute homes.

Those concerned with prevention - which included the Child Poverty Action Group, the National Council of One Parent families, Gingerbread, Mind and the British Association of Social Workers (BASW) - supported aspects of the Bill, such as the proposals to improve adoption practice and to clarify the standing of substitute parents. However, they opposed the government's intention to make permanence a central part of child care policy on a number of grounds. First, they argued that the permanency doctrine was based on false premises: the view that children could only be emotionally stable if placed with one set of parents was fallacious; moreover, social workers did not place undue emphasis on the 'blood tie', and the estimates of the numbers of children needing adoption was greatly exaggerated. Second, in spite of the compelling evidence linking poverty with entry to care, the Children Bill made no provision to improve the material conditions of parents most vulnerable to losing their children. Third, the Bill placed natural parents at a great disadvantage when compared with adopters and local authorities.

Even so, the Bill became the Children Act 1975, and child care policy appeared to shift towards concentrating on the removal of children rather than on the social disadvantages which put them at risk in the first place. Holman (1988) argues that a historical comparison can be made between the permanency movement and child emigration in the days of the British Empire. Both took children from poor families and placed them with more affluent ones, both ignored the adverse effects of cutting children away from their biological roots, and both gave little consideration to reforming social conditions in order to help parents retain their children.

During the 1970s, SSDs were subject to further investigations into child abuse, which resulted in a pervasive fear among social workers of 'a Maria Colwell happening here'. This, together with the permanency doctrine, changed social work practice. In response to a DHSS circular, most SSDs established child-abuse registers and area review committees; they also initiated special training for social workers. In addition, many Departments devised programmes to operationalise permanency. Specialist fostering and adoption units were created to find permanent homes for 'children who wait'. SSDs also appeared readier to assume parental rights, with the number of resolutions in England and Wales rising from 12,000 in 1973 to 18,400 in 1979 (Holman, 1988). Thus, by the end of the decade, a higher proportion of parents had lost their say in their children's lives than at any other time - including under the Poor Law.

Such trends inhibited prevention in at least three ways: (i) they depressed social work enthusiasm for prevention; (ii) they were accompanied by a medical model of casework which did not fit easily into preventive approaches; and (iii), SSD's gave less priority to prevention when allocating resources.

Throughout the 1980s, however, pressure groups highlighted cases where natural parents had suffered injustices and campaigned for more positive preventive action. These groups included: One Parent Families; the Family Rights Group (formed in opposition to the Children Bill); and consumer organisations such as Justice for Children and Parents Against Injustice (PAIN). Further, in 1983, social workers formed a Special Interest Group in Prevention and Rehabilitation in Child Care within BASW. The case for prevention was also made by official reports. In 1980, the Conservative Government asked the National Institute for Social Work (NISW) to set up a committee of inquiry to review the role and tasks of social workers. The ensuing Barclay report, named after the committee's chairperson, Peter Barclay, was published in 1982.

The Barclay Report clarified the nature of social work, justified its value, and recommended ways by which to improve its practice. Echoing Seebohm, the Barclay Report's central theme was that SSDs should practice community social work; that is, social work which seeks to tap into, support and underpin local networks of formal and informal relationships. No organisational blue-print was put forward, but the Report argued that community social work would be more accessible to the public and would make greater use of local resources than the existing system (NISW, 1982).

A minority report written by a sub-group led by Professor Roger Hadley argued that the implementation of community social work necessitated more than just a change in social work attitudes. Hadley proposed that all SSDs should decentralise into area teams covering up to 30,000 people, with 'patch teams' of social service staff covering up to 10,000.

But the idea of community social work was rejected by one member of the Barclay Committee, Professor Robert Pinker, and also received a mixed reception outside. Concerned with upholding social work standards, Pinker doubted whether local communities could sustain patterns of informal care as an alternative to professional help. He contended that the patchwork model of organisation would jeopardise the future of social work and mobilise groups for political ends; or, conversely, be used to generate informal help in order to justify drastic cuts in statutory funding. Pinker maintained that the existing model of social work was basically sound, but required a more clearly defined and less ambitious role. He envisaged the professionalisation of social work, with the establishment of a general council for social work and highly trained social workers. Rather than concentrating on communities, Pinker considered that social work should be reactive rather than preventive and modest in its aims, for it had neither the capacity, resources nor mandate to seek out need in the community.

9

However, Holman (1988) countered that the Barclay Report did, in fact, acknowledge the limitations of community social work; second, that none of its members sought to set in motion a process that could become a framework for political extremists of either left or right; third, that experiments in community social work known prior to the Barclay Report indicated that communities do possess helping networks which social workers could stimulate and tap; fourth, that such experiments did not support the view that a neighbourhood approach was not acceptable to those in need, that it endangered privacy or that it extended state intrusion; and, fifth, that far from diminishing social work skills, neighbourhood-based work appears to enhance them.

Nevertheless, Pinker succeeded in weakening the case for SSDs to have a broad preventive role. At a time of severe cut-backs in welfare spending, Pinker's argument for restricting preventive work seems to have found favour. This may help to explain why the Barclay report was not implemented by central government.

The Children Act 1989

Immediate origins

Unlike the Barclay Report, which addressed a wide range of social work matters, the inquiry initiated by the Social Services Committee of the House of Commons and chaired by Renee Short MP, was specifically concerned with vulnerable children and their families. The inquiry resulted from growing debate about the rights of children, on the one hand, and the rights of parents, on the other; and concern about the decisions being made for deprived children. The Short Report, published in 1984, embraced many child-care issues. However, the major theme of the report was the need to improve preventive services for children and families; indeed, it made more recommendations about this than any other topic, and even exceeded the emphasis placed on prevention by Seebohm. The Short Report also made its mark as the first official document to question the doctrine of permanency. The report argued that the stress on permanency had resulted in neglect of policies and practices which either enabled parents permanently to look after their own children or to maintain links with them while in long-term care.

Short and her colleagues lamented the lack of a concerted strategy to prevent children from entering long-term care; a shortcoming which the report attributed partly to a lack of organisational commitment to prevention by managers to parallel that which they gave to adoption and fostering; partly to the lack of priority accorded to prevention by social workers; and partly, to the reluctance of society to see money spent to uncertain effect on 'socially incompetent families', despite the fact that much greater sums are less grudgingly devoted to rescuing the victims of such circumstances (House of Commons, 1984).

The Short Report advocated the development of services such as child-minders and daily foster care to support vulnerable parents in coping with their own children. The Report called for changes in legislation to protect natural parents, such as the abolition of local authorities' powers to remove parental rights without a court hearing; it also wanted to see a duty placed on local authorities to rehabilitate all children in their care, and not only those admitted under voluntary procedures. In addition, the Report added its weight to the notion of a family court as the appropriate place for making far-reaching decisions about the lives of children.

In response to the Short Report's call for ...'a major review of the legal framework of child care'...., the government set up an interdepartmental committee which, in 1985, published a *Review of Child Care Law* (DHSS, 1985). Although it omitted any consideration of family courts and primary poverty, the Review followed the Short Report in emphasising prevention. For example, it called for a more positive approach to prevention with less emphasis on keeping children out of care and more on local authorities having a broad power to provide services to promote the care and upbringing of children by their families. To this end, it supported the concepts of 'respite care' and 'shared care'. Second, the Review also concurred with the Short Report that the local-authority power to assume parental rights should be abolished, which would mean that any compulsory removals would have to be through the courts. Third, various changes were advocated with the aim of reducing the number of children in care - for example, the Review recommended that non-school attendance should no longer be a sole ground for making a care order, and that restrictions should be placed on the use of Place of Safety Orders and Interim Care Orders. Fourth, the Review stated that, unless contrary to the interests of children looked after by local authorities, the latter should have a duty to return them to their families.

The *Review of Child Care Law* and the Short Report reflect an important change in the official thinking that had dominated the Children Act 1975. The 1975 Act had focused on legislation to remove children; the later documents concentrated on the need to enable parents to keep or receive back their children. The *Review of Child Care Law* and the Government White Paper which followed - *The Law on Child Care and Families Services* (House of Commons, 1987) - paved the way for the Children Act 1989.

However, it would be misleading to imply that all the factors which helped to shape the public law components of the Children Act 1989 appeared to support the case for greater emphasis on keeping families together. Throughout the

1980s, SSDs were subject to continued pressure concerning child abuse. Official investigations, particularly those into the deaths of Tyra Henry and Jasmine Beckford, led to more criticism that social workers were failing in their duty to protect children from dangerous parents. Both investigations stressed the need for adequate measures to protect children (London Borough of Brent, 1985; London Borough of Greenwich, 1987). Yet, around the same time, a series of research projects commissioned by the Department of Health stressed the need for partnership with parents, and the concepts of respite care, shared care and rehabilitation; they also highlighted the inappropriate use of compulsory powers by local authorities (Department of Health and Social Security, 1985). Moreover, the inquiry into arrangements for dealing with child abuse in Cleveland, reinforced the view that measures were needed to safeguard the rights of parents. The Cleveland Report made a number of recommendations, including that Place of Safety Orders should only be sought for the minimum time necessary to ensure the protection of the child (Department of Health, 1988).

Of course, protecting children and safeguarding the interests of parents are not mutually exclusive aims. The case for prevention is not one that seeks to undermine efforts to stop cruelty to children or to hinder social workers in their desire to plan carefully for children's futures. Rather, the point is that such activities need to occur within the context of a high commitment to prevention and the promotion of the social conditions and social services that enable parents to look after their own children. The Children Act 1989 wisely seeks to balance the need to protect children and the necessity of safeguarding the interests of parents.

Aims and principles

The main aims of the Act include making the law relating to children easier to understand, simpler to use, more consistent across different situations, but also more flexible both in terms of what can be achieved and the means by which objectives can be met. The Act also seeks to render the law more appropriate to the needs of children. Thus, it promotes services for, and decisions about, children, young people and their families that are more child centred than was the case under the old law (Open University 1990).

A number of key principles underpin the Act. For example, the notion of 'parental rights' is replaced by the concept of 'parental responsibility', which emphasises the obligations of parents towards their children. However, the Act also recognises that parents may need support in fulfilling their responsibilities. Thus, previously restricted notions of 'prevention' are superseded by 'family support', and local authorities have a new duty to facilitate the upbringing of children by their parents. Partnership between parents and local authorities is accordingly promoted. Local authorities cannot assume parental righ\ demand notice of a child's removal from 'accommodation'; rather, they must work on a basis of negotiation and voluntary agreements. Where negotiation fails, and children are removed, parents must be kept fully informed and only exceptionally denied access to their children.

The Act places the child at the centre. The child's welfare is paramount and must be considered in the context of his or her physical, emotional and educational needs, age, gender, background and the capacity of caregivers to perform their task adequately. Further, when resort is made to the legal process, the latter must be speeded up. Emergency Protection Orders must be of short duration and courts must work to timetables to avoid children suffering the adverse consequences of delay. In addition, the child's voice must be heard. Children's wishes and feelings must be determined and taken into account when decisions are made. A balance is sought between children and parents, the state and families, courts and local authorities, and, where power is unequal, the Act tries to safeguard the weak. Hence, the needs of children come first because of their dependence and vulnerability, but parents and other significant adults are given increased respect and consideration (Packman and Jordan, 1991).

The 1989 Act makes specific reference to race, culture, language and religion as factors to be considered in relation to the welfare of children. The Act places a new duty on local authorities to take account of the different racial groups to which children in need belong when contemplating the provision of day care or accommodation. This point is reinforced in respect of day care. Section 74 (6) states: 'In considering the needs of any child ... a local authority shall ... have regard to the child's religious persuasion, racial origin and cultural and linguistic background.' The Department of Health's (1989), *The Care of Children, Principles and Practice in Regulations and Guidance*, highlights the special issues that arise for black children and young people and those from ethnic minority groups. It affirms that such children need to develop a positive self image which includes their cultural and ethnic origins, and that this must be taken into consideration by service planners and caregivers.

Children in need and their families

Under s.1 of the Child Care Act 1980, local authorities had a duty to diminish the need to receive children into, or keep them in, local authority care. However, the concept of family support introduced by the Children Act 1989 is much broader. Under s.17 of this Act, local authorities have a general duty to safeguard and promote the upbringing of children in need. To this end, they must facilitate the upbringing of children by their own families, and must provide services, including accommodation, for such children. Services must

13

also be provided for the family of a child in need. Provision of accommodation for a child should not be viewed as failure by the family or the social worker. The term 'family' includes anyone with parental responsibility and anyone the child is living with (White et al., 1990).

Prior to the implementation of the Act, Department of Health Guidance stressed that: (i) services should be provided in a non-stigmatising way; (ii) provision of services should enhance the authority of parents; (iii) children should participate in decision making; and (iv) service provision should be sensitive to the needs of ethnic minority communities (University of Leicester and Department of Health, 1991). The Act gives local authorities considerable scope to offer services to improve children's lives by, for example, providing opportunities for play and pre-school learning, preventing family breakdown and helping to maintain links for children separated from their families.

However, targeting services on children in need is intended to be a proactive, rather than a reactive task. The Act requires local authorities to identify the extent to which there are children in need in their area, publish information about their services, and facilitate the provision of services by others. Local authorities are therefore required to develop strategies and systems which seek out children in need and encourage children and families to come forward (White et al., 1990).

Under s.17 of the Act, children are in need if they require local authority services to achieve or maintain a reasonable standard of health or development, or they need local authority services to prevent significant or further impairment of their health and development, or they are disabled. A child is disabled if he or she is blind, deaf, dumb, or is suffering from any mental disorder, or is substantially or permanently handicapped by illness, injury or congenital deformity or other such disability as may be prescribed. Development is widely defined to encompass physical, intellectual, emotional, social or behavioral development; and health means physical and mental health. Yet the Act gives no clear indication of what is to be understood by a reasonable standard of health and development, or by significant or further impairment. These matters must be judged with reference to all other children in the local area, not only those who live in a similar, and possibly quite disadvantaged, community to that of the child in question.

It is evident that the definition of need contained in the Children Act is wide enough, potentially, to embrace all children who could be helped by the provision of services. Yet, it does not indicate which children or families should be given priority nor generally, the types of services that should be provided (University of Leicester and Department of Health 1991). However, the Act does refer to a variety of services that may be necessary to support families, including: advice, guidance and counselling; occupational, social, cultural or

14

recreational activities; home helps and laundry; travel to services; holidays; family centres; accommodation for children and families; accommodation/cash assistance for re-housing abusers; assistance in kind; cash assistance (exceptional circumstances only); and day care, out of school, and holiday activities (Schedule 2; s.17 and s.18). In addition, the Act permits local authorities to facilitate the provision of services by others (s.17).

Local authorities were required to comprehensively overhaul their existing child care policies and strategies before the Act was implemented. Many already had policy statements and guidance based on the old legislation. However, the trend towards restrictive, residual policies in recent years has meant that previous definitions, criteria and standards probably fell short of the new requirements, both in terms of level of services (now more positive) and range of services (especially including disability). Limited resources have obliged local authorities to establish priorities, based on studies of local needs, and re-allocate resources amongst services.

Although local authorities have wide discretion to determine the range and level of services, the Act includes specific powers and duties which give some indication of the purposes for which family support services should be provided. These are: the prevention of ill-treatment and neglect, the reduction of the need to bring care or related proceedings, the reduction of delinquency and criminal proceedings against children, minimising the effects of disability on children with disabilities, and the promotion of family re-unification and contact (Schedule 2).

There is also broad agreement on a number of categories (not mutually exclusive) of children who should be regarded as in need within the terms of the Act. These include: children with disabilities; children at risk of abuse and neglect; children who are delinquent, or at risk of becoming so; children separated from their parents because of divorce, separation, hospitalisation, parent in prison, immigration restrictions, and so on; children being looked after by local authorities; children with caring responsibilities (e.g. teenage parents, children of parents with disabilities); children whose home conditions are unsatisfactory - for example, those who are homeless, in temporary or substandard accommodation, or in accommodation for homeless families; and children who may be broadly defined as living in poverty and at high risk of family breakdown, (University of Leicester and Department of Health, 1991).

Gardner and Manby (1993) have observed that the social justice definition of need (as opposed to the individual pathology definition) recognises the inequalities inherent in society, on the basis of which whole areas rather than individual families could be defined as needy. These authors also refer to the working group, co-ordinated by Jane Tunstill at the National Council of Voluntary Child Care Organisations (NCVCCO), which set out the basis by which need could be assessed in a holistic way using the powers as well as the duties set out in the Act. However, pressures on family support have increased since then which makes it more likely that the individual pathology definition of need will continue to be predominant.

Summary of key points

In this chapter we have outlined the historical process whereby the narrow concept of 'curative' prevention espoused by the Victorian system of child welfare has developed - albeit by fits and starts - into the much broader spirit of proactive family support enshrined in the Children Act 1989. The Victorian system of child welfare was class based, stigmatising, and emphasised 'rescue' and 'fresh start', rather than prevention and rehabilitation. Parents were seen to be the cause of the problem, which meant that the cure necessitated permanently separating them from their off-spring. Indeed, the concept of rehabilitation did not reach the statute book until the Children Act 1948 was passed following the Second World War. Together with the social welfare legislation of the 1940s, which reduced poverty and contributed towards full employment, decent housing and improved health, the new Children's Departments created by the 1948 Act also provided impetus for preventive work. The latter was further fuelled by the Ingleby Report in 1960. Recommendations from the Report were given legislative expression in Section 1 of the Children and Young Persons Act 1963. This extended the work of the Children's Departments from a curative rescue service to one whose role was to promote the welfare of children by working with the whole family; a goal which was further pursued by the unified Social Services Departments created at the beginning of the 1970s on the recommendation of the Seebohm Report.

However, the tragic death of Maria Colwell, and research evidence suggesting that substantial numbers of children were being allowed to 'drift' in care, led to calls for renewed stress on removing children permanently from their parents. The Children Act 1975 appeared to reverse child care policy and practice in the direction of removing children rather than addressing the social disadvantages which put them at risk in the first place. Against this, however, the Barclay Report, published in 1982, rekindled the notion of community social work earlier advanced by the Seebohm Report. But the Barclay Report received a mixed reception both within and outside social work and was not implemented by central government.

Yet, not long afterwards in 1984, the Short Report placed unprecedented emphasis on the need to improve preventive services for vulnerable children and their families. This Report also called for a major review of the legal framework of child care law, which led to the Children Act 1989. The Act rightly seeks to balance the need to protect children with the need to safeguard the interests of birth parents. The concept of family support contained in the Children Act is a revolutionary step forward from the old, restricted notions of prevention. Under the Act, local authorities are given a far more positive, outreaching, responsibilities for children in need and their families.

Appropriately, therefore, our next chapter will look at agency policy with regard to fulfilling these obligations.

2 Agency policy

In theory at least, the services we provide to vulnerable children in our society are determined by policy. When we write a policy statement, we are describing our intentions and philosophies. The Children Act, for example, makes it clear that services to families should be more child-centred than they were before: partnership with parents should be sought, and primary preventative efforts should be stressed.

Whether or not these things actually occur, at least central government policy exists to say that they *should* occur. Conversely, at the local authority level, and particularly at the level of family and children's services departments, policy statements rarely seems to be in place.

As mentioned in the last chapter, the issues discussed in this book follow directly from the results of a study on the ways in which social services departments (SSDs) are implementing Part III of the Children Act. In this chapter, we will look at three key issues: the importance of writing goals into policy documents, with particular reference to defining the concept of 'children in need'; problems associated with identifying children in need; and children with disabilities.

Writing goals into policy documents

At the beginning of the study, the researchers examined the policy documents of the eight SSDs in Wales and eight comparative SSDs in England. They found that policy documents concerning children in need varied considerably in length and content. Some were brief, containing no reference to many of the duties required of local authorities by Part III of the Children Act, while others were comprehensive, covering almost every duty. A second associated finding, arrived at after examination of what SSDs were actually doing, was that in general, the documents did not do justice to the efforts and achievements of social services departments with respect to the implementation of the Children Act. In other words, SSDs appear to have taken the spirit of the Children Act to heart and are attempting to comply with its requirements, even though they may not state in their policy documents that they have any such intention. It might appear that this does not matter much. Provided that they are doing the right thing, what does it matter whether or not they have made a formal statement of intent?

There are three possible problems with the what-does-it-matter philosophy. First, there is the danger that they may not continue to do the right thing. Staff come and go. Informal ideas about what ought to be done and how will change over time, and the gap between the original intention and the eventual intention may widen out of all recognition if the original intention was never written down. For example, take the complaints procedures. The Children Act requires SSDs not only to develop a formal complaints procedure but to publicise it so that clients and everyone else involved will know what it is and can make use of it if necessary. Suppose that a particular SSD does develop a complaints procedure and does publicise it, and the result is an overwhelming number of relatively trivial complaints which all have to be dealt with at considerable time and cost. Harried managers might almost be forgiven for deciding that the word 'publicise' need not necessarily mean 'make public'. Instead, it might mean instructing social workers to make the complaints procedure known to clients *if* and *only if* the social worker feels that the client has genuine grounds for complaint.

This modified, gate-keeping form of publication may gradually become the norm: and it is not unlikely that the change will be made slowly, without fanfare, so subtly in fact that few people realise a change has occurred. The first problem, then, is that a policy which is never written down may change over time, in ways that are not only unplanned but may not even be discussed.

Even if the policy itself remains the same, the way that it is carried out may not, and this brings us to the second problem: the difficulty of monitoring a policy which has never formally existed. In theory, monitoring is a simple business. First, we have a policy, through which we express our goals: our intentions and philosophies - what it is we want to accomplish, and why. Second, we have procedures: the actions we plan to take in order to reach our goals. Third, we have activities: the actions we practically take, which may well differ in subtle or not-so-subtle-ways from the actions we had planned. Fourth, we undertake monitoring: a careful, objective review of the first three things.

When we monitor goals, for example, we might ask whether our goals are appropriate to the people we are serving and realistic in light of the social, political and economic context in which they will have to be achieved. If we decide that there is nothing wrong with our goals, we can move to a review of our procedures. Were the actions we planned to take logically likely to lead to goal achievement? If they were, we can progress to our activities. To what extent did we do what we planned to do? In what ways did we deviate from the plan, and why? Once we have established that we followed a plan of action which should have led to goal achievement, we can turn our attention to evaluation. *Did* our plan of action lead to goal achievement? To what degree have we achieved our goals?

This is theoretically a simple process which can help us to identify practical problems. For example, publicising a complaints procedure is not a goal: it is an *action*, taken by an SSD in order to achieve some goal, as yet unspecified. Thus, it is not particularly useful for an SSD to write in its policy document that it intends to publicise its complaints procedure. The point that policy must address is the reason behind the publication: the goal that publication is intended to accomplish.

Suppose that this goal is to enable all persons who are dissatisfied with the service they have received to have their concerns objectively addressed within three months from the date of the complaint. The wording of the goal leads logically to certain actions. First, some sort of a procedure must be developed - the complaints procedure - through which concerns can be objectively addressed. The word 'objective' in itself dictates, to some extent, the nature of the procedure: there will need to be an independent judge. Next, the procedure must be publicised in a way that will reach all potentially dissatisfied persons, taking into account the fact that some clients may be reluctant to pick up leaflets because they do not read very well, or they do not read English very well. Then, a monitoring procedure must be put into place, so that we can establish whether an appropriate complaints procedure exists, whether potentially dissatisfied persons are aware of it, and how well it works within the specified time frame: to what degree, in short the goal is being met. Finally, the results of the monitoring process must be used to identify problems and to try to resolve these problems by modifying the publication procedure, or the complaints procedure or possibly even the goal.

None of these things can occur if there is no goal: if it has not been specified in the policy document exactly what it is that the department hopes to accomplish. We now have two reasons why goals need to be written into policy: first, written goals are less likely to change over time in an unplanned way than unwritten, informal goals: and, second, goal achievement cannot be measured unless there is a formal goal. The third reason has to do with consistency in practice within and between departments.

It seems to be human nature to make comparisons - or perhaps it is social conditioning, but, whatever it is, there is no doubt that people tend to compare the way they are treated with the way other people are treated. Not only that, they compare the way they are treated now with the way they used to be treated when they lived somewhere else and were served by a different SSD. If SSDs

20

have written goals and written procedures for accomplishing these goals, comparisons can be drawn, and efforts can be made to achieve a reasonable consistency nation-wide. Similarly, at the departmental level, written goals and procedures make it less likely that different departments within the same bureaucracy will be independently using their different methods to struggle towards their different, and sometimes conflicting, goals. Finally, and possibly most importantly, the existence of written goals and procedures will allow individual social workers to know where they stand. They will know what they are supposed to be doing and why, and, since they will all be given similar guidance, it becomes more likely that different clients in different places will be treated similarly - with a possible resulting increase in client satisfaction, and a concomitant decrease in the number of submissions made to the (now well-publicised we hope) complaints procedure.

We now have three reasons for expressing goals in writing in policy statements. Since they appear to be relatively good reasons, we must wonder why SSDs seem to be so loathe to do just that. One reason is undoubtedly the time and cost involved. Writing goals, together with the associated procedures, is a delicate and time-consuming business, particularly when the goals must be co-ordinated within and between departments, and attention is required from high-level staff. However, the particular endeavours to which time and money are devoted are always a matter of priorities. We are left with the inference that managers do not consider the formulation of goals to be a priority, and again we must ask, Why not?

One possible answer may simply be that social services staff in general tend not to think in terms of management through the pursuit of goals and objectives. It may even be that they deliberately avoid bringing to bear on social work the kinds of techniques that work so well in business because they believe - quite rightly - that social work is not a business: its philosophies and goals are different. However, there is no real reason why some of the strategies developed by for-profit organisations might not be modified for use by the public sector.

Suppose, for example, that a restaurant chain is considering building a new restaurant, with the simple goal of making a profit of a million pounds over the space of, say, a year. The first step in the process will be a needs-assessment: an attempt to match the services provided by the restaurant to the needs of the potential clients in order to determine where the restaurant might best be built. If the chain specialises in providing fast, cheap food to teenagers and parents with small children, then it will build its restaurant in an area where people are not rich enough to scorn it, nor too poor to patronize it, and where there are liable to be lots of teenagers and small children: in a middle-class district, between an elementary and a high school, for example. We may be sure that, before a stone is laid, chain managers will know what population they are proposing to serve, what the needs of the population are, and how the service will be provided, at what closely-estimated cost. They would not consider possibly providing the wrong kind of service to a population they had not identified, at un unknown cost, in a location which may be inaccessible to the people being served. Far less would they consider failing to monitor the level of their goal achievement. Yet social service departments do this all the time. It is perhaps not unreasonable to ask whether a higher goal than profit justifies the abandonment of the eminently sensible strategies which for-profit organisations commonly employ.

However, a reluctance to associate themselves with business methods is probably not the only reason, or even the primary reason, why social services managers have avoided formulating goals. The primary reasons may lie in the nature of the goals themselves and the commitment to goal achievement inherent in formal expression. For example, if an SSD writes in its policy document that it intends to ensure equality of service to ethnic minority groups. and it writes in its procedures manual that it will achieve this goal through the provision of ethnically-sensitive play equipment in day-care facilities, through translation services, and through the active recruitment of ethnic minority staff, carers and foster parents, then it leaves itself open to evaluation on the basis of these criteria.

Perhaps managers in an area where the ethnic minority population comprises two per cent of the whole (which is the case in some Welsh counties) privately believe that it is not worth going to great expense to provide translation services for the use of so very few. Perhaps, indeed, they are not able to provide translation services because translators are unavailable. Whether or not the initial belief is justified, it may not be politic to express it: and managers may not wish to be told that translators *could* become available if greater efforts were made to establish positive relationships with ethnic minority communities. The issue here is motivation: specifically the desire to avoid expressing goals which managers may not be able to achieve without an expenditure which, in their eyes, is unjustified.

Another associated issue is confusion: doubt in the manager's mind about what the goal is that ought to be expressed. A good example of this lies in the problems presently being experienced by SSDs in defining 'children in need'. The Children Act defines the concept of need as follows:

...a child shall be taken to be in need if:-

> (a)   he is unlikely to achieve or maintain, or have the opportunity
> of achieving or maintaining, a reasonable standard of health

and development without the provision for him of services by a local authority under this Part;

(b)   his health or development is likely to be significantly impaired, or further impaired without the provision for him of such services; or

(c)   he is disabled.

The words 'disabled', 'development' and 'health' are themselves more completely defined in the Act, but there is no precise definition of the phrases 'reasonable standard of health and development' or 'significantly impaired'. According to Department of Health guidance on the Act, the definition of 'need' is left deliberately wide to reinforce the emphasis on preventative support and services to families. While this move towards prevention is much to be applauded, it is also apparent that the given definition includes all children who could potentially benefit from the provision of services: more children than any local authority could practically serve.

Local authorities are thus presented with a dilemma: whether to define 'children in need' in a narrow sense, including only obvious and specific populations, such as children already in care or children at risk of abuse or neglect; or whether to widen the definition to include other categories of children, such as those whose current, relatively minor problems are likely to worsen over time without appropriate intervention. If they choose the former, they are running counter to the broad spirit of prevention enshrined in the Act. If they choose the latter, they are essentially promising a service they may not practically be able to deliver. Their other choice, of course, is not to choose: to simply write in their policy documents that they will provide the appropriate service to 'children in need' as defined by the Act.

Study findings show that they are choosing not to choose: and the result of that is that social workers on the front line are obliged to decide for themselves which children are eligible for what particular service. Since opinions among social workers vary widely, children in similar situations tend to be treated differently, with the inevitable consequence that comparisons are made, blame is apportioned, and resentments are fanned.

We might note here that 'providing a service to children in need' is not a goal any more than 'publicising a complaints procedure' is a goal. Both of these are actions undertaken by departments in order to reach a goal. The question departments need to ask in order to formulate the goal is Why should a service be provided to children in need? What purpose will be served by providing such a service? If the answer is that children will be prevented from coming into care, then this answer in itself has defined what is meant by 'children in need'. 'Children in need' are children who would be taken into care without the provision of preventative services. On the other hand, if the answer is that children will be enabled to enjoy, in their own homes, the kind of parenting, the freedom from suffering, the standards of living, and the quality of community life which is considered reasonable for children in our society, then 'children in need' comprise a much broader population. It is clear that 'children in need' must be defined before a goal can be written, and the difficulty of arriving at a definition is one obvious reason for the failure to formulate the goal.

So far, then, we have said that policy documents rarely contain service goals, partly because goals have a business flavour, and partly because managers do not want to commit themselves in writing to goals which may be politically unpopular, financially unattainable or undesirable in any other way. We have also said that the practice of not writing goals leads to inconsistency in service (since social workers must make their own independent and widely varying decisions), an absence of the monitoring procedures which might result in problem-solving and improvement, and a real possibility that goals will alter in an unplanned way. The ways forward that obviously follow from these findings are:

1. Policy documents should contain written goals around every aspect of the Children Act.
2. An effort should be made to ensure that these goals are consistent within and between departments.
3. Goal statements should cover all client populations (for example, ethnic minority groups), no matter how small these groups may be in relation to the whole.
4. Policy documents stating goals should be accompanied by procedures manuals which lay out actions intended to achieve the goals.
5. Social workers should receive formal guidance on both goals and procedures.
6. A monitoring system should be put into place whereby checks are made to ensure that goals are appropriate, actions are being carried out as planned, and the planned actions are leading to goal achievement.

At the end of the chapter, we will present a list of key points and associated ways forward, but it is probably useful to identify them first as we go along. Let us turn now to the matter of identifying children in need.

Identifying 'children in need'

We have talked about the difficulties of defining 'children in need', and these difficulties lead on to yet more difficulties when we come to think about providing service to them. Children cannot be served until they have been identified - until we know who they are and where they are to be found. The matter of who they are (which is still a question of definition) has been addressed by the Department of Health and the University of Leicester who have together come up with eight categories. Children might be said to be in need if they are:

- at risk of sexual abuse;
- at risk of other forms of abuse or neglect;
- delinquent or at risk of becoming so;
- separated from their parents;
- living in families suffering from serious problems;
- living in inadequate home conditions (such as bed and breakfast accommodation);
- living in poverty; or
- disabled.

The matter of where they are to be found involves deciding whether we should wait for them to come to us or whether we should go out and look for them. In light of the fact that SSDs are struggling to cope with the numbers of children referred to them, it does not seem very sensible to suggest that they should go out and look for more. However, some categories of children are more likely to be referred than others, and if we only serve those who are referred, we are automatically assigning priorities to the different categories. For example, children at risk of abuse or neglect will be referred as soon as they are discovered; and delinquent children will doubtless come to the attention of social services far more readily than children who are merely poor.

The consequence of restricting service to referrals is therefore likely to be that we focus our efforts on children who are already having problems rather than on children who need our help to avoid having problems in the future. In other words, the focus is on protection rather than prevention; and the consequence of *that* will inevitably be that we will be obliged to protect in the future those children to whom we fail to provide preventative service now.

Study findings show that this is precisely what is happening: and the problem is compounded by the fact that social workers tend to think in protection terms when deciding whether or not a child is in need and what services ought to be provided. One reason for this is doubtless a lack of resources. Social workers

25

seem to believe - with some justification - that there is little point in identifying a need which cannot be met. Children living in poverty, for example, comprise a much broader and more nebulous group than children at risk of abuse. There is relatively little that social workers can do about hard-core poverty, but there is quite a lot they can do about potential or actual abuse. They therefore tend to define a 'need' as a need they can do something about.

If the only children to be identified as 'in need' are those children who can currently be helped, it follows that children for whom there are presently no resources never will be helped. Further, since these children have not been identified as being in need (because they cannot be helped), it will not be possible to estimate the additional amount of money required to serve them.

This is obviously a no-win situation; and the reality is not as bad as that, although it makes a close approach. Under the Children Act, departments are required to assess the degree to which there are children in need in their area, and they have all put varying amounts of effort into accomplishing this. Most have made use of child protection registers to furnish information on the numbers of children suffering from sexual abuse, and from physical or emotional abuse or neglect. However, far fewer have information on the numbers of children in other categories of need, particularly children living in inadequate home conditions or in families suffering serious problems. The difficulty of identification is compounded by the fact that vulnerable children move in and out of being in need: they can fall simultaneously into several different categories of need and may also be identified by several different agencies and hence be counted a number of times.

Here again, the figures most commonly available are figures around protection cases - because these data have been collected, because these children are being served. Data on children who are being less adequately served have less often been collected: hence, in order the acquire the necessary information, departments have to engage in new assessment studies. Some departments have done this by setting up interagency working groups, undertaking specific research projects, and carrying out audits of need. However, most have not, and the argument once more is that it is not worth spending large amounts of money to identify children whose needs the department will not be able to fulfil.

The same argument has been applied to producing cost estimates. Few departments have estimated the cost of providing service to children identified as being in need: and those who have not tend to see the whole performance as an exercise in futility. What is the point, they ask, of knowing that there is a shortfall of millions of pounds when none of the necessary pounds will ever be provided? It cannot be denied that there is truth in this, but there is also some truth in the argument that money is even less likely to be provided if no-one knows how much is needed, and how much would be spent on what were some to be forthcoming.

Ordinary budgetary juggling also demands some estimate of how much present and potential social services programmes cost to run. Peter cannot usefully be robbed to pay Paul without a knowledge of how much Paul needs and how much Peter has. Managers who have suggested that child and family services do not have a sufficiently high political profile to attract adequate funding have also stated that better use could be made of existing funding if resources were reallocated within their departments and resources supplied by other statutory and voluntary agencies were more appropriately used.

In sum, then, we have said that, despite the emphasis in the Act on preventative services, the focus in practice is still very much on protection. Social workers tend to define a child as being 'in need' only if they feel they have the resources to meet that need. In the same vein, estimates of the numbers of children in need are largely based on existing data, which have to do with the numbers of children already being served. New assessment studies are rarely undertaken on the grounds that it is not worth while to identify children whose needs cannot be met, and cost estimates are rarely produced for similar reasons. The ways forward from these findings are probably fairly apparent:

1. Social workers should be encouraged to decide whether or not a child is 'in need' on the basis of the child's situation, regardless of the availability of resources to meet the need.
2. Departments should not measure the extent of need by making a count of demands already presented. Rather, they should carry out new assessment studies, preferably in co-operation with other statutory and voluntary agencies.
3. When new data are collected for any reason (for example, a review of services for children under eight), attention should be paid to collecting the data in a form that will enable them to be used for general needs-assessment purposes.
4. Estimates should be produced of the costs of running existing and potential social services programmes.
5. In an effort to shift the balance from protection to prevention, current budgeting arrangements should be examined. For example, because of the Children Act trend towards fewer applications for care proceedings and fewer children in care, it may be possible to recycle resources trapped in fixed capital costs and turn these into available revenue.

Let us turn now to children with disabilities.

Children with disabilities

Under Schedule 2 of the Act, local authorities have specific duties to children with disabilities. They must maintain a register of such children; and they must provide services designed to minimise the effects of the disability and permit the child to live as normal a life as possible. However, the Act also clearly states that a child with a disability is first and foremost a child, and therefore the primary aim should be to promote access to the same facilities as those available for other children.

The main dilemma here is that services appropriate to children without disabilities may not be suited to disabled children by reason of their disability. In departments where the focus is on providing a broad range of services for all children, it is often the case that children with disabilities cannot access some of the services and so have a limited choice. A common solution is to provide key areas of service for all children in need plus additional services for children with disabilities. Key services generally provided are: general social work support in the form of advice, guidance and counselling; day care and respite care, which includes sponsored child minding, nurseries and playgroups; accommodation in the form of fostering and adoption; and occupational, social, cultural and recreational activities, including such things as play schemes, youth clubs and support groups. Additional services for children with disabilities include a far greater level of respite care, aids and adaptations, and specialist teams set up to work with children and their families.

Some departments have also realised the importance of improving their links with other service providers, including the voluntary agencies. For example, plans are under way in one department to develop what is termed as a 'one stop shop for services' in co-operation with the health and education authorities.

The matter of identifying children with disabilities is proving more problematic. Some departments are able to provide information on the total number of disabled children in their area, but very few have data on the numbers of children in separate categories of disability: for example, blind, deaf, congenital deformity, mental disorder, and so forth. The main source of the difficulty appears to be poor liaison and communication with other agencies, such as health and education. The education authority has historically been responsible for special needs children, and there is client group specialisation for mental handicap and the blind and the deaf. They all have their separate registers, and the problem now is how to integrate services.

It may be argued that the primary problem is not how to integrate services but how to manage interagency endeavours in general. We will discuss this problem in more detail in chapter 6.

Another problematic issue is the register for children with disabilities. Study findings show that approximately half of the departments examined have set up registers and the other half are working on getting their registers running, usually in co-operation with the health and education authorities. While registers have been set up, however, the accuracy of the information contained in them is doubtful.

Department of Health Guidance points out that to have maximum value the register must be complete and must avoid duplication with other registers. Avoiding duplication is a prime reason for co-operation between agencies, but now confidentiality becomes an issue, since service users providing information to one agency may not have intended that it be shared with others. A further difficulty lies in the fact that many children who fall within the disabled category will have been statemented under the Education Act 1981. However, there will be some who have not, and there will also be children who have been statemented but who will not fall into the disabled category under the 1989 Children Act.

The matter of completeness is also quite complex. Parents are not required to register their children, and some parents are reluctant to do so because they perceive that inclusion in the register may carry a stigma and lead to little benefit. Some departments are trying to change this view by presenting registration as a gateway to services: an action that may spring from worthy motives but throws some doubt on the extent to which registration is really a matter of choice. Registration as a 'gateway' implies that some services lie beyond the gate and will be denied to those who do not choose to register: a form of persuasion which may be effective but is certainly unethical.

A more ethical but probably less effective method of encouraging parents to register their children is to try to reduce the perception of stigma through public relations exercises. Public perception of social services is often negative, mainly because of the association of social work with child protection work. This association, fuelled by media interest in child abuse cases, inevitably stigmatises both the users and providers of social services, and is likely to discourage parents of disabled children from having anything to do with a social services register. It may well be the case that publication of information about the full range of services available to parents and children would reduce the association with protection and promote a new appreciation of the positive aspects of prevention. However, old associations die hard: and such an endeavour would doubtless require a more compelling presentation than a summary of services from a social worker or the production of an explanatory leaflet. This may be an occasion when the media's interest in social services could be used to some advantage.

In sum, we have said here that SSDs appear to be striking an appropriate balance between providing specialist services to children with disabilities and giving them access to general programmes and facilities. Identification of children in specific categories of disability is proving problematic, largely because of poor liaison between social services and the health and education authorities. Another difficult matter is the register for children with disabilities. Avoidance of duplication requires interagency co-operation and raises confidentiality issues, while the requirement that the register be complete means that effective and ethical ways must be found to persuade parents to register children. In light of this, the following ways forward might be considered:

1. Departments should be encouraged to provide services for children with disabilities in co-operation with other agencies, particularly the health and education authorities.
2. Data should be collected on the numbers of children in specific categories of disability.
3. All departments should be encouraged to set up registers of children with disabilities, in co-operation with the health and housing authorities, and to provide estimates as to completeness. (e.g., there are 200 children on the register but it is estimated that 250 will need to be served.)
4. Caution should be used in presenting registration as a gateway to services, since such a strategy may be perceived to contain a coercive element.
5. An alternative strategy to encourage registration may be an attempt to reduce the perception of stigma by publicising, in an arresting manner, the full range of preventative services available to families and children.

We will end this chapter with a summary of findings, together with the associated recommendations, presented in point form as an aid to clarity. In the next chapter, we will explore the ways that social workers view some of the key issues arising from the Children Act.

SUMMARY

Formulating goals

Key points

Policy documents rarely contain service goals. The practice of not writing goals leads to inconsistency in service, an absence of monitoring procedures, and a possibility that goals will alter in an unplanned way.

Ways forward

- Policy documents should contain written goals around every aspect of the Children Act.
- An effort should be made to ensure that these goals are consistent within and between departments.
- Goal statements should cover all client populations (for example, ethnic minority groups), no matter how small these groups may be in relation to the whole.
- Policy documents stating goals should be accompanied by procedures manuals which lay out actions intended to achieve the goals.
- Social workers should receive formal guidance on both goals and procedures.
- A monitoring system should be put in place whereby checks are made to ensure that goals are appropriate, actions are being carried out as planned, and the planned actions are leading to goal achievement.

Identifying 'children in need'

Key points

Despite the emphasis in the Act on preventative services, the focus in practice is still very much on protection. Social workers tend to define a child as 'in need' only if they feel they have the resources to meet that need. In the same vein, estimates of the numbers of children in need are largely based on existing data, which have to do with the numbers of children already being served. New assessment studies are rarely undertaken on the grounds that it is not worth while to identify children whose needs cannot be met, and cost estimates are rarely produced for similar reasons.

Ways forward

- Social workers should be encouraged to decide whether or not a child is 'in need' on the basis of the child's situation, regardless of the availability of resources to meet the need.
- Departments should not measure the extent of need by making a count of demands already presented. Rather, they should carry out new assessment studies, preferably in co-operation with other statutory and voluntary agencies.

- When new data are collected for any reason (for example, a review of services for children under eight), attention should be paid to collecting the data in a form that will enable them to be used for general needs-assessment purposes.
- Estimates should be produced of the costs of running existing and potential social services programmes.
- In an effort to shift the balance from protection to prevention, current budgeting arrangements should be examined. For example, because of the Children Act trend towards fewer applications for care proceedings and fewer children in care, it may be possible to recycle resources trapped in fixed capital costs and turn these into available revenue.

Children with disabilities

Key points

SSDs appear to be striking an appropriate balance between providing specialist services to children with disabilities and giving them access to general programmes and facilities. Identification of children in specific categories of disability is proving problematic, largely because of poor liaison between social services and the health and education authorities. Another difficult matter is the register for children with disabilities. Avoidance of duplication requires interagency co-operation and raises confidentiality issues, while the requirement that the register be complete means that effective and ethical ways must be found to persuade reluctant parents to register their children.

Ways forward

- Departments should be encouraged to provide services for children with disabilities in co-operation with other agencies, particularly the health and education authorities.
- Data should be collected on the numbers of children in specific categories of disability.
- All departments should be encouraged to set up registers of children with disabilities, in co-operation with the health and housing authorities, and to provide estimates as to completeness. (e.g., there are 200 children on the register but it is estimated that 250 will need to be served.)
- Caution should be used in presenting registration as a gateway to services, since such a strategy may be perceived to contain a coercive element.

\-   An alternative strategy to encourage registration may be an attempt to reduce the perception of stigma by publicising, in an arresting manner, the full range of preventative services available to families and children.

3 Need assessment

In the last chapter, we talked about the importance of writing goals into policy statements and setting out the associated action plans in procedures manuals. However, even the best policies and procedures will not be effective in improving service without the understanding and co-operation of the social workers who are supposed to implement them. In this chapter, therefore, we will look at the views of administrators and front line social workers about the strengths and limitations of the Children Act as it affects service to children in need in practice.

Defining children in need

As we mentioned in the last chapter, the definition of need in the Act covers three categories of children: children who are not likely to maintain 'a reasonable standard of health and development' without services; children whose health and development are likely to be 'significantly impaired' without services; and children with a disability. This definition is broad enough to include any child who could potentially be helped by the provision of services: more children than SSDs could practically serve.

When researchers asked 103 front-line social workers whether they thought the definition was adequate, opinions were split essentially in half. Just over half considered that the definition of need provided in the Act *was* adequate. The main reason given was that a broad definition is flexible: it does not really exclude any child and it allows social workers virtually unlimited freedom to decide who might best be served in what particular way.

Conversely, just under half considered that the definition was a 'cop out': a woolly definition which allows SSDs to avoid making any specific commitment to provide service to any group of children. The argument here is that, instead of letting more children in, as the legislators intended, the very breadth of the Children Act definition is in fact keeping more children out, since SSDs now have no clear, legal obligation to provide any particular service to any particular child.

In general, lead child care managers and principal officers agreed that the definition was a cop out. They also agreed that they have a responsibility as administrators to make the definition less woolly by providing guidance to social workers on how such phrases as 'reasonable standard of health and development' and 'significant impairment' ought to be interpreted in practice. What is meant by 'reasonable'? How significant is 'significant'?

Some managers admitted that they were reluctant to provide guidance because it would involve them in a profound dilemma. If they instructed social workers to interpret the terms in a broad sense, they would be committing themselves to meeting the needs of more children than they could practically afford to serve. If, on the other hand, they set down a narrow interpretation, they would be blatantly contravening the spirit of the Act. If they avoided the dilemma and allowed social workers to make their own interpretations, they were essentially condoning the inconsistencies in service that must result when one social worker arrived at a broader interpretation than another.

At the time the interviews were conducted, two years after the Children Act came into force, just under half of the SSDs examined were avoiding the dilemma. A lead child care manager in one did not perceive a dilemma. He saw additional guidance as unnecessary, remarking that there was already adequate information available to social workers in the form of Department of Health guidance, books, and other publications produced outside the department. It might be noted that this information was originally intended to provide guidance in the area of protection, and we will come back to this point later in the chapter.

Some managers said that they had provided guidance, but the next obvious questions - What guidance? What did you say? - revealed the existence of yet another difficulty with definitions. What *is* guidance? What kinds of information do departments have to provide - and how - before they can be said to have issued guidance? Should they hold a meeting, or a training workshop, or recommend a book, or pass round a pamphlet? Must they address the meanings of 'reasonable' and 'significant' or is it enough to give a general lecture on assessment skills: what social workers ought to look for when assessing a child as being 'in need'?

Before we delve into the nature of guidance, it might seem reasonable to lay down one basic criterion: guidance has only been issued if the social workers concerned are aware that they have been guided. On the basis of this criterion, none of the departments who said they had issued guidance had in fact provided it, since approximately three quarters of the social workers interviewed did not remember any. Of those who did remember receiving it, some could not remember what it was, while others said that they had received course handouts or brief notes or instruction from a field work manager; or they had been referred to the child protection manual, or read some books that the department had distributed.

In light of this, it is probably safe to assume that social workers have not received guidance: and we should turn our attention instead to what they are doing in practice without it. There are essentially three answers to this: some are seeking guidance from other sources, primarily the child protection literature: some are relying on assessments of need made by workers from other agencies, usually health visitors; and some are using their own experience, as parents and as social workers. Most, of course, are doing all three. In addition, as might be expected, nebulous ideas about what 'in need' means in theory are beginning to harden, moulded by the kinds of children who are perceived to be needy in practice. Practice is leading theory, rather than the other way around.

It might be useful to examine the consequences of this more closely. First, it probably means that nothing much has changed as a result of the Act. Social workers are continuing to do pretty much what they always did, and the longer they continue to do it, the less likely it is that change will occur in the end. Tradition, as we have said before, dies hard. Second, the probability that change will occur in the direction of prevention - in the event that it occurs at all - falls ever lower as more social workers rely for guidance on the child protection literature. A mindset is being established, and such a mindset, taken together with the fact that more resources are expended on protection than prevention, may well result in an inadvertent shift away from the spirit of prevention towards the 'heavy' end of child care social work.

The nature of this mindset is most evident in social workers' own interpretations of what is meant by 'reasonable standard of health and development' and 'significant impairment'. The vast majority said in interview that they defined 'reasonable standard' in terms of whether a child was reaching developmental milestones and receiving adequate basic care. Adequate basic care was usually deemed to include, in no particular order: sufficient warmth, food, and health care; adequate clothing, appropriate to the weather and also to the child's age; adequate and appropriate education; a basic level of hygiene; adequate housing; and 'the odd cuddle'. Reaching developmental milestones was defined both in terms of the social worker's own experience - achieving what you would expect of a child that age - and on the basis of tests and indicators used by colleagues in the health care field: for example, Centile charts, to measure height and weight in relation to age; and the Ruth Griffiths test, a test designed to examine the intellectual development of a child aged under five.

Social workers' ideas of adequate basic care tend to centre on material aspects such as food and warmth which are common to any culture. However, attention is also paid to the adequacy or otherwise of the parenting being provided: that is, assessments are made not only on the basis of the child's actual developmental level but on the basis of whether the care being provided could be expected to *result* in an adequate developmental level, in the social worker's opinion. Since ideas about what does and does not constitute adequate parenting tend to vary widely from culture to culture, social workers need to be particularly sensitive to cultural differences when they are making assessments on this basis. In the same vein, assessments based on whether the child is 'achieving what you might expect from any child' assume that the child's culture and the social worker expect the same thing - an assumption which may not always be justified.

Naturally, predictions about the difficulties which might arise from a child's current situation lie at the very heart of preventive work. Social workers cannot assess whether a child is 'likely to achieve' a reasonable standard of health and development without making judgements about the adequacy of the environment in general and the parenting in particular. Neither can they assess whether his development is 'likely to be' significantly impaired without making a similar judgement.

When asked how they would define 'significantly impaired', a quarter of the social workers interviewed said directly that a child who was 'significantly impaired' was one who was being abused or neglected. Most of the rest gave criteria opposite to those they had given previously with respect to 'reasonable standard'. Children were 'significantly impaired' if they were *not* receiving adequate basic care, or *not* reaching developmental milestones: if, in short, they were failing to reach a 'reasonable standard of health and development' as the social worker had defined it.

So far, then, we have seen that social workers are essentially split 50-50 with respect to whether they think the definition of need given in the Act is adequate. Administrators tend to think it is not adequate, agree that they have a responsibility to issue guidance regarding it, but have not generally done so to date. In the absence of guidance, social workers are deciding themselves how a child 'in need' should be defined: and differences in their opinions mean that there is little consistency in service between and within authorities. In addition, two distinct, though not mutually exclusive, lines of thought seem to be currently prevalent among social workers: first that 'reasonable standard' and 'significant impairment' are opposite sides of the same coin; and, second, that a child who is 'significantly impaired' is one who is in need of protective services. One major recommendation follows from these findings:

1.   If it is departmental policy to move away from an emphasis on protection towards proactive prevention, then procedures for accomplishing this must be specified. Such procedures might include:

(a) Discourage social workers from using protection material to guide them in preventive work by issuing alternative guidance designed to emphasize prevention;

(b) Develop guidance materials in co-operation with other statutory and voluntary agencies;

(c) Establish indicators for prevention work along the same lines as the *Working Together* material (Home Office et al., 1991) has established indicators for protection;

(d) Formally issue the guidance in joint training sessions together with other statutory and voluntary agencies.

Identifying and prioritising children in need

Since we dealt with identifying children in need in the last chapter, we will touch on it only very briefly here, as a prelude to discussing prioritisation. As we have seen, practice is leading theory with respect to defining and identifying children in need. Social workers do not identify children as being 'in need' on the basis of some theoretical definition of need. Rather they develop their own definitions on the basis of which children they would practically identify as needing to be served: and these children tend to be children in need of protective services for whom resources can be made available. In other words, social workers are establishing their own priorities - priorities which definitely lean towards protection and away from proactive prevention.

In order to clarify the prioritisation issue, lead child care managers and social workers were asked to rank nine categories of children in two ways: first, in order of the actual service priority each category was presently receiving; and, second, in the order which each category should ideally have. This exercise, undertaken in phase 1 of the study, was repeated one year later in phase 2.

The categories presented for ranking were those mentioned in the last chapter:

- children at risk of sexual abuse;
- children at risk of physical/emotional abuse and neglect;
- children who are delinquent or at risk of becoming so;
- children leaving care;
- children with disabilities
- children separated from their parents;
- children with serious family problems;

- children whose home conditions are unsatisfactory; and
- children living in poverty.

With respect to 'actual' service priorities, the way that children were ranked presented no surprises. Highest priority was being given to children at risk of abuse or neglect: and, indeed, emphasis was generally being placed on the six categories of children for whom local authorities have a clear statutory responsibility. These are the first six categories appearing on the list above: children at risk of sexual abuse; children at risk of physical or emotional abuse and neglect; children who are delinquent or at risk of becoming so; children leaving care; children with disabilities; and children separated from their parents.

With respect to ideal rankings, social workers and managers were far more likely to give equal ratings to most of the categories, reflecting a desire to give equal priority to all children's needs. Failing an equal priority, the ideal was to move away from simply prioritising child protection towards putting more emphasis on areas which might reduce the need for statutory intervention. For example, children living in poverty, who were ranked last in actual priority, moved up to fifth place in the ideal ranks, while children with serious family problems similarly moved from seventh place to fourth.

Somewhat surprisingly, children separated from their parents came last in the ideal rankings. It was not, of course, that social workers did not consider this group of children to be important. Rather, they believed that, by putting more resources into other areas such as serious family problems and poverty, they would address the separation problem by reducing the number of children in this category. The same reasoning applied to the 'delinquency' group which came third in the actual rankings but fell to seventh place in the ideal.

By phase 2 of the study, both actual and ideal rankings had changed in a way that the researchers found disturbing. Children separated from their parents were being ranked third in actual priority (as opposed to sixth in phase 1), and third in ideal priority (as opposed to ninth in phase 1). This increased attention to separated children may reflect the possibility that there are an increasing number of children in this category: a possibility which cannot be verified since, as discussed in the last chapter, virtually no statistics are available. It may also indicate that efforts to address the problem of separated children indirectly through preventive work have either not been made, due to insufficient resources, or have not borne fruit, so that more attention must now be given to providing services directly.

In this same vein, it is interesting to note that poverty, ranked fifth in the ideal ratings in phase 1, had dropped to the eighth place in the ideal ratings by phase 2. Either social workers were assigning less importance to poverty as a category of need, or they were growing more sceptical of the possibility of addressing poverty, even in a relatively ideal world. It might also be noted that children with disabilities, though a statutory responsibility, had dropped from fifth to seventh place in the actual rankings between phases 1 and 2. Indeed, the ideal in phase 2 was to restore children with disabilities to the priority they had actually been receiving in phase 1.

When team leaders were asked which of the nine categories of children would be most likely to remain unallocated longest, their responses not unnaturally reflected their 'actual' priorities. They indicated that children at risk of abuse and neglect were dealt with immediately and did not remain unallocated. Those most likely to remain unallocated were children living in unsatisfactory home conditions and children living in poverty.

Much the same picture emerged when lead child care managers, team leaders and social workers were asked to assign actual and ideal ranks to levels of prevention. A useful model developed by Hardiker et al. (1991) identifies four distinct levels of prevention. First level prevention or 'diversion' is directed towards vulnerable groups, communities, individuals and families and is geared towards empowering families and strengthening their own support networks rather than creating dependency on social services. Second level or 'early' prevention is directed towards families in temporary crisis: that is, towards those whose difficulties are not so great that there is a high risk of family breakdown or whose difficulties were of a higher order but are being resolved. The aim here is to bring about changes in circumstances so that intervention is no longer necessary and the case may be closed. Third level, or 'heavy-end' prevention is directed towards families with chronic problems, where there is a high risk of family breakdown, neglect or abuse, or where the child has recently been returned home from local authority accommodation. The purpose of intervention is to maintain the gains made or improve the situation so that agency input can be reduced. Finally, fourth level intervention or 'early restoration' is directed towards children being looked after by the local authority in order that these children may be returned home if this is consistent with their welfare.

Rankings showed that 'actual' first priority was given to families with chronic problems, where children were at risk, and second priority was afforded to children presently being looked after by the authority. Families in temporary crisis came third while proactive preventative work with vulnerable families and groups came last. Ideally, managers agreed that children at risk must have first priority, but reversed the order of the other three categories, placing proactive prevention work second, families in temporary crisis third, and children being looked after last. As an aid to clarity, these results are tabulated below.

	Actual Ranking	Ideal Ranking
1st level, diversion	4th	2nd
2nd level, early prevention	3rd	3rd
3rd level, heavy-end prevention	1st	1st
4th level, restoration	2nd	4th

Again, these results show that actual priority is being given to the 'heavy' end of child care work, though social workers and their managers would prefer to give more emphasis to diversion and prevention. Recommendations following these findings seem hardly appropriate since there is already a great deal of frustration among social services staff over their inability to expend their limited resources in the way that they would like. Instead, we will move on to examine a related bone of contention - the adequacy of service provision in the context of family support.

Family support services

While the Children Act does not require that any particular type of service should be provided to children in need or their families, it does suggest the kinds of services that may be appropriate. These services comprise: advice, guidance and counselling; occupational, social, cultural, or recreational activities; home helps and laundry; travel to services; holidays; family centres; accommodation for children and families; accommodation/cash assistance for rehousing abusers or suspected abusers; assistance in kind; cash assistance (exceptional circumstances only); and day care, out of school and holiday activities.

However, in practice, local authorities have wide discretion in determining the range and level of services that may be provided under Part III of the Act. In order to gain a clearer picture of actual service provision, social workers and lead child care managers were asked to state whether they felt that provision was adequate or inadequate for each of the family support services listed above.

It was evident from the responses given that lead child care managers and social workers had different opinions about the adequacy of some of the services available. The services most likely to be thought adequate by managers were home helps and laundry, and accommodation or cash assistance for rehousing abusers. However, only 16 per cent of social workers felt that home helps and laundry were adequate; and only 24 per cent believed that adequate assistance was provided to abusers. A significant minority, (22 per cent in each case) did not know whether these services were adequate or not since they had never had occasion to put them to the test. The services most likely to be thought adequate by social workers were counselling and cash assistance.

Generally both managers and social workers felt services to be inadequate, and mostly they agreed as to which services were least adequate. Services deemed to be least adequate were: family centres; occupational, social, cultural or recreational activities; accommodation for children and families; and day care, out-of-school and holiday activities.

Managers and social workers were next asked which categories of children they felt were most affected by inadequate services. Not surprisingly, the children least likely to be affected by inadequate services were felt to be children at risk of abuse or neglect. However, a number of social workers did suggest that lack of services affected these children as well: examples cited were lack of counselling and support for sexual abuse victims and their families, and lack of service after leaving care. Leaving care was one of the areas in which opinions differed, managers believing that these children were relatively well served, and social workers believing them to be the group which suffered most.

The categories of children identified by both social workers and managers as most likely to be affected by inadequate services were children living in poverty, children in unsatisfactory home conditions, and children with disabilities. When asked whether they felt that the available services were adequate in general, the overwhelming majority of social workers (95 per cent) said that they were not.

Some social workers made additional comments about the needs of other groups of children: those from a minority cultural background, for example, or those living in rural areas. With respect to cultural background, they stressed that more emphasis should be placed on targeting ethnic minority communities when recruiting foster parents so that culturally appropriate foster homes would be available when needed.

Children living in rural communities were thought to confront the additional problem of isolation. Families often live some distance from the location of services, in areas where public transport is infrequent and expensive. The problem is exacerbated by the weak voluntary base that exists in many rural areas, resulting in an increased reliance by vulnerable families upon difficult-to-access social services. Social workers felt that a number of initiatives could be put into operation: for example, relocating certain services; developing resources within rural areas; and introducing mobile services, such as play buses.

Most social workers, however, were pessimistic about the possibility that such initiatives could actually be undertaken in the current economic climate. They understood very well that a resource, once available, is more likely to be offered, or indeed demanded by knowledgeable service users. The very fact that a need can be met is liable to uncover more people with that need than had formerly been imagined. To some extent, then, more need is revealed by the very act of meeting need, and managers are obliged to take this into consideration when deciding what services they are practically able to provide.

Although we will be discussing parents' points of view in the next chapter, it is probably worth noting here the services that parents said they wanted social workers to provide. The service most frequently requested was advice, guidance and counselling: a catch-all sort of service which covered a wide range of problem areas. Specific problem areas most often mentioned included: help with disciplining children or with disturbed, violent or disabled children; emotional support and befriending; school-related issues; obtaining injunctions or restraining orders against a violent partner; restricting or gaining custody or access; support for the siblings of children receiving services; pre-natal support for pregnant teenaged children; and respite care in the form of short-term accommodation, day care or baby-sitting services. As we will see in chapter 5, children also identified unmet needs, mostly emotional but also material.

In sum, then, we have said that actual service priority is being given to the 'heavy' or protection end of child care work, even though most social workers and managers believe that the only way to reduce the heavy end is to pay more attention to the lighter or prevention end. It is thus hardly surprising that those categories of children accorded lowest priority - children living in unsatisfactory home conditions or in poverty - were also those deemed to be most likely to suffer from inadequate services. It follows, in addition, that the services found to be least adequate are the very services which would be most likely to assist these children: for example, family centres; occupational, social, cultural or recreational activities; and day care, out-of-school and holiday activities.

We might offer a few recommendations based on these findings:

1. The adequacy of the following services might be investigated: occupational, social, cultural or recreational activities; accommodation for children and families; and day care, out-of-school and holiday activities.

2. Greater emphasis might be placed on family centres, which the study found to be one of the services least adequately provided.

3. The feasibility of the following initiatives might be studied, with respect to improving service in rural areas: relocating certain services; developing resources within rural areas; and introducing mobile services, such as play buses.

As before, we will conclude the chapter with a summary of key points and ways forward before moving on to look at parents' views in chapter 4.

SUMMARY

Defining children in need

Key points

1. Social workers are interpreting the concept of need in a wide variety of different ways, with little agreement as to how a child 'in need' should be defined.

2. Despite the wide variety of individual definitions, two distinct, though not mutually exclusive, lines of thought seem to be currently prevalent among social workers: first that 'reasonable standard' and 'significant impairment' are opposite sides of the same coin; and, second, that a child who is 'significantly impaired' is one who is in need of protective services.

3. In the absence of adequate guidance on the concept of need, social workers are turning for guidance to material that was primarily formulated for use in child protection work. The danger here is that dependence on such material may result in an emotional and intellectual move away from the broader themes of need and family support towards protection issues.

4. In addition to the use of child protection material, social workers are relying on their own experience, both as social workers and as parents. The criteria used most often to decide whether a child is 'in need' are whether the child is reaching developmental milestones and whether the child is receiving basic adequate care.

Ways forward

1. If it is departmental policy to move away from an emphasis on protection towards proactive prevention, then procedures for accomplishing this must be specified. Such procedures might include:

   (a) Discourage social workers from using protection material to guide them in preventive work by issuing alternative guidance designed to emphasize prevention;

   (b) Develop guidance materials in co-operation with other statutory and voluntary agencies;

44

(c) Establish indicators for prevention work along the same lines as the Working Together material (Home Office et al., 1991) has established indicators for protection;

(d) Formally issue the guidance in joint training sessions together with other statutory and voluntary agencies.

Identifying and prioritising children in need

Key points

1. Lead child care managers and social workers were asked to rank nine categories of children in two ways: first, in order of the actual service priority each category receives; and, second, in the order which each category should ideally have. 'Actual' rankings indicated that SSDs are clearly concentrating their efforts on children at risk of abuse and neglect. However, when asked how they would prioritise under ideal circumstances, managers and social workers were far more likely to give equal ratings to a number of categories, an indication of their desire to give more emphasis to preventative work so that fewer children would be in need of statutory intervention.

2. Social workers, team leaders and managers would all ideally wish to give more priority to children with disabilities and less to delinquent children.

3. With respect to allocation of cases, children at risk of abuse or neglect are dealt with immediately and do not remain unallocated. The two categories most likely to remain unallocated are children living in unsatisfactory home conditions and children living in poverty.

4. With respect to service provision, both managers and social workers feel that services are generally inadequate. The services deemed to be most adequate are counselling and cash assistance, while those thought to be least adequate are: family centres; occupational, social, cultural or recreational activities; housing for children and families; and day care, out of school and holiday activities.

5. Children least likely to be affected by inadequate service provision are children at risk of abuse or neglect, although some of these children would also be included in the 'sexually abused' and 'leaving care'

45

categories, for whom services are thought to be inadequate. Children most likely to be affected are children living in poverty, children in unsatisfactory home conditions, and children with disabilities.

Ways forward

1. The adequacy of the following services might be investigated: occupational, social, cultural or recreational activities; accommodation for children and families; and day care, out-of-school and holiday activities.

2. Greater emphasis might be placed on family centres, which the study found to be one of the services least adequately provided.

3. The feasibility of the following initiatives might be studied, with respect to improving service in rural areas: relocating certain services; developing resources within rural areas; and introducing mobile services, such as play buses.

4 Working in partnership with parents

In the last chapter, we discussed some of the difficulties encountered by social workers in providing service to 'children in need' and their families under the Children Act 1989. In this chapter, we will look at the services provided from the point of view of the parents receiving the service; and, in the next chapter, we will go on to examine the children's perspective.

One of the new concepts to emerge from the Children Act 1989 is the idea of 'parental responsibility' which, according to the Lord Chancellor, Lord MacKay, '...runs through the Act like a golden thread, knotting together parental status and the effect of orders about a child's upbringing...' As defined in the Act, parental responsibility means 'all the rights, duties, powers, responsibilities and authority which by law a parent of a child has in relation to the child and his property'. In tandem with parental responsibility, the local authority has a general duty to promote the upbringing of children by their families, insofar as this is consistent with the children's welfare, by providing a range and level of services appropriate to the children's needs. In other words, the duty of the local authority is to form a partnership with parents wherever possible to support them in the exercise of their responsibility.

It is worth looking at this matter of parental responsibility a little more closely. One of the most sensitive issues to beset a welfare state operating in a democratic society is the degree to which the state should interfere in the private lives of families for the purpose of ensuring the welfare of one or more of the family members. Domestic violence is now a police matter. Husbands are not permitted to beat their wives, nor parents their children, nor adult children their elderly parents. With respect to violence, we have decided as a society that the state has a right to override family privacy in order to safeguard the weak.

Along with rights must come responsibility. If the state has a right to safeguard a child from being beaten, then the responsibility for a child who has been beaten must surely be the state's. So far, we are on relatively safe ground. Few social workers would deny that, as servants of the state, they have a duty, as well as a right, to remove an abused child from the home and provide an alternative form of care which will best serve the interests of the child.

However, we also currently believe that the interests of the child will be best served, in the long term, if the child can be raised by the natural parents in the family home. Hence, removal is a last-ditch resort and all efforts are made, once the child is in care, to work with the parents so that the child can be safely returned. Two points might be noted here. First, the responsibility for the child's safety still lies firmly with the state, as evidenced by the furore that arises if a returned child later comes to harm at the parents' hands. Second - and possibly incidentally - the theory that a child is best looked after at home fits nicely with the present thrust towards reducing welfare costs.

The state's responsibility also holds good with regard to the grosser forms of neglect. Parents are not permitted to fail to provide their children with adequate food, clothing and shelter; and the state will provide these things in the event that the parent cannot. Warmth, as an aspect of shelter, appears to be a more nebulous matter. The material for this chapter is derived from interviews with parents and children, which happened to be conducted in the winter, in homes where the heating was, for the most part, non-existent, inadequate, sporadic or unsafe. It may be that the state does, indeed, accept responsibility for providing families with a safe and adequate source of warmth and is merely failing to fulfil its responsibilities in this regard: or it may be that such things as broken or unsafe radiators are viewed by SSDs as the parents' responsibility and not the state's.

The same ambivalence seems to apply to other safety hazards. Is it the state's responsibility to repair a broken stair-rail which may endanger the safety of a two-year old? What about a loose stair carpet, or a rat's nest, or rusting debris in a yard, or a broken garden gate? None of the parents who pointed to these things appeared to feel that they should deal with them themselves: in their view, the responsibility for their children's safety lay firmly with the state.

While it is obviously absurd to suggest that SSDs should be directly responsible for every household hazard, assistance to parents to enable them to cope themselves may be a more feasible proposition. As social workers are only too well aware, the majority of the families on their caseloads live in communities which are highly disadvantaged, both materially and from the point of view of social isolation. These are usually not communities where the neighbours are prepared to rally round to lend a tool or share a skill or volunteer labour. Rather, they consist of socially isolated households whose members have few friends, are estranged from family, and tend to have difficulty forming relationships because of unfortunate past experiences: people whose self-esteem, already low, is further eroded by living in what can only be called a slum.

Some social workers are trying to remedy this situation by providing paint and other decorating materials, often wielding a brush themselves while discussing family progress. However, much more could be accomplished through community development efforts based in family centres. Community-based centres can not only provide multi-disciplinary social services in a more accessible and less intimidating setting: they might also act as a meeting-place for residents and as a focus for concerted community effort facilitated by social workers.

We have said then that, while SSDs assume responsibility for abused and grossly neglected children, there are greyer areas in which parents believe that responsibility belongs to the state and the state, in the form of SSDs, believe it belongs with the parents. Let us move on now to look at two other issues in which responsibility is also a matter for contention: truancy and delinquency.

When asked about their primary concerns in relation to their children, parents put truancy at the top of the list. They associated non-attendance at school with all kinds of other problems such as delinquency, drug abuse and sexual activity, and showed a great deal of frustration with the inability of social workers to remedy the truancy problem. Most parents thought that SSDs should have more power than they apparently did over school-based decisions such as transfers and suspensions; and some parents believed that the social worker did in fact have such power but was refusing to exercise it on their behalf.

Suspensions were seen as a 'cop-out' because many children did not object in the least to being suspended and some, indeed, had worked towards this end. Transfers were viewed more positively since children tended to do well in special placements, but problems invariably occurred when the placements were terminated and the children returned to the local school. One mother said that, after her 14-year old son's return from a special placement and his subsequent expulsion from the local school, he had been provided with a home tutor for an hour a day, which 'gave him the rest of the day to get into trouble'. While quite willing to admit that her son was a difficult student, she did not see why the combined forces of the social services, the education - and often the police - departments should have failed to get him back to school.

Much of the difficulty seems to revolve around communication. Parents are often reluctant to talk with teachers and believe that social workers should act as intermediaries between the family and the school, the police and the school, and the special and local schools. One parent was angry that her daughter had been suspended for misbehaviour on the day before she was to make a video telling how she had been sexually abused as a child. According to the parent, it was the social worker's job to inform the school beforehand of the situation or, failing that, at least to get the suspension lifted.

Be this as it may, there is no doubt that many parents are intensely frustrated by the seeming inability of any authority to enforce the law regarding school attendance. Frustration often reaches its highest pitch when something positive seems to have been accomplished - a child does well in a special placement, say

- and then the intervention ends, there is a lack of follow through, the gains are lost, and the child is worse off than before. Most schools are willing to involve parents if the parents wish, but there are many parents who, because of their own past experiences, are not able to co-operate with teachers in such matters as explaining the child's home situation, or adapting for use in the home behaviourial strategies which have worked at school, or talking to the teacher in the local school about the child's experience in the special school. Support from the social worker in initially co-ordinating such efforts might go a long way towards alleviating school-related problems while, at the same time, empowering the parent and improving child-parent-school communications.

The second concern most voiced by parents in relation to their children was delinquency. Here, parents were just as frustrated by the social worker's inability to solve the problem but were less prone to blame either the worker or the department. They were not themselves able to control their children and in general understood why no-one else was able to either. The majority believed that their children would end in prison and, in many cases, this sense of inevitability seemed to be accompanied by an anticipatory feeling of relief: a prison sentence would mean a temporary end to their responsibility.

It is especially, perhaps, in the area of out-of-control children that the balance between parental and societal responsibility comes most into question. When the parent cannot cope, the child is often accommodated and social workers make efforts, in tune with current policy, to place the child as close as possible to home so that family links may be maintained. Children in close proximity to home tend to go home, particularly if they have some difficulty with the foster home - not being allowed in, for example, when the foster parents are out - or if they have achieved a position of power in the natural home, and are able to obtain money or vent rage or gain some other satisfaction denied them in the foster home.

Some parents are physically afraid of their children, both on their own behalf and with respect to their younger children. Others are less afraid of physical assault than of damage to the house itself and to its furnishings. Still others are concerned about the influence on siblings of a child who is violent, abusing drugs or in trouble with the law. In short, for many parents, the family ties that are being maintained are just a continuance of the destructive relationships which led to the child's accommodation in the first place.

Parents often feel that they are being blamed: first, for the child's delinquent behaviour; second, for their inability to control the behaviour; and third, for their expressed reluctance to have the child back home. Some said in interview that the social worker seemed to pay them no attention when they asked that the child should live further away, or visit home less often. Rather, the result of these requests was that they were labelled as unco-operative or hostile: 'bad' parents, from whom a plea for help was viewed as a measure of their own incompetence. A few had already had their children returned despite their protests, and they saw this as a 'cop-out' on the social worker's part: an abrogation of the state's responsibility for children with whom it too had failed to cope.

Social workers would be the first to admit that there exists a core population of children with behaviourial disturbance for whom no placement or intervention seems to be effective. Many of these children desire to go back home - perhaps because they are most powerful at home - and the Children Act, which places the child at the centre, does expressly state that the child's wishes must be taken into account. The child's expressed desire, together with the emphasis on parental responsibility and the maintenance of family ties, makes it almost inevitable that parents who do not feel able to accept their responsibility will have their wishes overruled. We might ask here whether the child's wishes should so often take precedence, or even whether the child's welfare should always be our prime consideration in cases where the child's proximity to home will threaten the welfare of other family members.

This focus on the child is also evident in the differential treatment of the accommodated child with respect to non-accommodated siblings. Many parents with accommodated children felt strongly that these children were receiving goods and services which were denied to their siblings left at home; and that the situation was exacerbated by visits from the accommodated child during which possessions and privileges were flaunted before the other children. Since accommodation was often the result of criminal activity, parents believed that bad behaviour was essentially being rewarded while good behaviour on the part of siblings was being ignored.

Even when the child was not being accommodated, parents still felt that the child on the social worker's list was receiving too much attention at the expense of the other siblings. The child who 'had a social worker' not only received visits, outings and material goods but was possessed of a special status which tended to lead to family friction and resentment even in cases where the child was obviously a victim and had never been guilty of any offence. Some parents with disabled children, while grateful for the help they were receiving, felt that this help should be extended to their other children, whose 'normal' lives were being disrupted by their sibling's disability. In these cases, local authorities were fulfilling their obligation to minimise the effect of disabilities on disabled children but seemed to be taking almost no account of the effect of the disability on the family as a whole. The problems we are identifying appear to stem from two concepts which lie at the very heart of the Act: first, that the child's welfare should be paramount; and, second, that SSDs should form a partnership with parents for the purpose of supporting them in the exercise of their responsibility.

51

While social workers are already aware that the welfare of the child is usually best served by working with the entire family, it does seem that more emphasis needs to be placed on the *family* rather than on the child alone.

A related issue here is the emphasis which is still placed on protection, despite the thrust of the Act towards the provision of preventive service. The children whose welfare is being regarded as paramount are often those children who have already been identified as in need of protection: the siblings who are being ignored - according to their parents - are children who might not need to be protected in the future if appropriate preventive services were presently in place.

To take an example, some of the children interviewed mentioned quite openly that they were working towards getting themselves accommodated in order to enjoy the resulting benefits. These children are not being prevented from wanting to be protected; and nothing is more likely than that they will achieve their ambition in the end. A second example may be found in the number of pregnant girls who did not expect to be served until after the child was born. Meanwhile, they were living at home in a relationship with their parents which often, at best, was fragile; or they were living with their boyfriends. One mother, who admitted that her relationship with her daughter was poor, was still upset about the fact that the girl had moved in with an already abusive boyfriend because she had nowhere else to go. The daughter, in this case, was not the child named on the social worker's list, but the mother felt that social services ought to pay attention to other family members, especially when the problems were 'right under their noses' and would eventually become their concern.

On the one hand, the mother is undoubtedly correct in assuming that, if preventive service is not provided, the daughter's child will eventually need to be protected. On the other hand, the assumption that the daughter's situation will eventually become 'their' concern runs directly counter to the 'partnership with parents' concept in which the problem belongs to the parent and the role of the SSD is to help the parent solve it. Parents tend not to see pregnant daughters with whom they have a poor relationship as *their* problem: along with truancy, delinquency, drug abuse, and even child safety, this problem belongs to the state.

Another problem that ought to belong to the state, in many parents' minds, is the cost of supporting accommodated children who return on visits. Some parents told the interviewer that they could not afford to feed the child, but the real source of their dissatisfaction, also voiced by other parents, seemed to be the amount of assistance given by social services to foster parents: an amount that was viewed as unfair and disproportionate. One mother said that foster parents, with whom her son had stayed for less than a week, had been given a wardrobe - and sold it for a substantial sum, according the mother. Other parents mentioned beds, clothes, household appliances and amounts of money, all given to the foster parents in return for accommodating the child for a relatively short period of time, and not taken back when the child moved on. Several of the more disgruntled remarked that, if they had been given this kind of assistance, they could have kept the child with them: and one mother had calculated the amount owed her by the state, based on two sevenths of the foster parents' pay for each weekend the child had spent at home.

This distinction between foster and natural parents also arises when a child is being cared for by a legal guardian or a grandparent. Several of the parents interviewed were grandparents. All without exception felt that they would have access to many more services and benefits if they were fostering the children, and they said that the children were suffering because, as guardians, they did not receive the support that foster parents did. According to one grandmother, her grandson's orthopaedic shoes cost £60 a pair, he went through a pair a month, and she could not afford them on her widow's pension.

Be that as it may, it does seem to reinforce the idea that parents - and, by extension, grandparents and legal guardians - have a moral duty towards their children which foster parents do not share: and, therefore, foster parents ought to be paid for providing a service which parents should give for free. Many people might agree with this - just as many people might argue that foster parents should not be paid either because payment detracts from the caring, dedicated, and ideally charitable, nature of the foster service.

We might take up a great deal of space discussing the moral stature - not to mention the financial situation - of a mother who counts a weekend visit from her child in terms of pounds and pence. However, the fact remains that many parents do feel a great deal of resentment towards foster parents because of the financial gap which often exists between them. Not only are foster parents paid more: they usually *have* more to begin with and are thus able to provide the foster child with activities and treats which the natural parents are not able to match. Some parents are grateful that their children should have these advantages: others are hostile because they feel inferior to the foster parent, or the child prefers the foster parents' home, or the situation is unfair to siblings, or the child ceases to be accommodated and becomes resentful when the accustomed benefits suddenly stop. Whatever the reason, the resulting hostility is hardly conducive to the climate of co-operation in which foster parents, natural parents and social workers are all supposed to work together for the greater welfare of the child.

Here again, part of the problem is that the focus *is* on the child and not on the whole of the natural family. While it may be impractical to suggest that foster parents should 'adopt' a family rather than providing service to a child, some foster parents do already include siblings in activities and trips, and do tailor the nature of gifts so that siblings, and sometimes even parents, have a share. The vital relationship between foster and natural parents is mediated from the beginning by the social worker and will much depend on whether the social worker's primary focus is protecting the child or providing preventive service to the family as a whole.

One aspect of responsibility which is of great concern to parents is interference. Social workers assess families, with the unspoken threat always lurking in the background that the child might be removed if the assessment is unsatisfactory. In other words, social workers, as servants of the state, assume responsibility for the welfare of the child, and it is this responsibility which gives them the right to suggest changes in family lifestyle which might promote that welfare.

From the point of view of some parents, social workers are assuming the rights while abrogating the responsibility. These parents perceive the social worker as making moral judgements about everything from smoking to boyfriends to a messy house. Such comments as, 'She doesn't think he ought to live here', 'She doesn't like him coming round', 'She doesn't think I ought to smoke around the baby' were made with a mixture of nervousness and resentment by parents who were both afraid of being found wanting and angry that their habits were subject to inspection.

The parents who saw the social worker as interfering were generally those who did not believe that the social worker's visits served a useful purpose. From their point of view, the social worker was ineffective in dealing with such major issues as truancy, delinquency and drug abuse, and either could not or would not help them with their other problems. These parents cited a long list of unmet needs, mentioning most often: counselling for sexual abuse victims; increased amounts of respite care; nursery school provision; protection from persistent and abusive ex-partners: organised activities for children, such as play schemes, sports or trips; advice on legal, medical and financial matters; information about services and benefits, including services provided by community and voluntary organisations; assistance in obtaining child support payments; introduction to parent support groups; services for 16-18 year olds; and information about hyperactivity and behaviour management.

Undoubtedly, some parents will always complain about social worker interference, no matter how sensitive the social worker, and it is often these very parents who need the intervention most. Likewise, some parents will never be satisfied with any level of service, however adequate. Nevertheless, people do tend to be more willing to tolerate intrusion the more they think they are getting in return, and the more they feel they have participated in deciding what services ought to be provided.

In the present climate of fiscal restraint, it may be difficult to meet some needs, such as increased amounts of respite care or more activities for children.

54

However, something might quite feasibly be done about meeting requests for more information in specific areas and about perceived levels of participation.

With regard to information, study findings showed that departments often rely upon social workers to provide whatever information to parents they feel is relevant at the time. This method of disseminating information relies entirely upon the social worker's own knowledge base, which may be inadequate in certain areas. In addition, the social worker's knowledge base, no matter how adequate in fact, is liable to be judged by the parent on the basis of other, seemingly irrelevant criteria: the social worker's age, for example. Young social workers are often assumed to know less, not only about matters deriving from life experience but also about facts which, on the face of it, bear no relationship to age, such as agency procedures or available services. A second criterion for assessing the social worker's knowledge is comparison of the information given with that received by the parent from other sources: for instance, neighbours, other professionals, such as health visitors - and most particularly television.

Since no sensible social worker would want to compete with television, it might be worth our while to improve our dissemination of information by such methods as holding film shows and public meetings, producing leaflets for social workers to distribute on common problems such as drug abuse or hyperactivity, erecting information booths in shopping centres, and whatever else our imaginations can devise. If we can do this, we will not only comply with the requirement in the Children Act to publish information about services: we may go some way towards dispelling the notion that all SSDs do is to snatch children; and we may mitigate our intrusion into the private lives of individuals by at least providing them with the kind of information they want to have.

With respect to having parents participate in decision-making, study findings show that many parents already feel they do. Some of the less contented did remark that voluntary care was essentially the same thing as a care order, since they did not believe that their children would have been allowed to stay at home had they not agreed to voluntary care. Nevertheless, most of the parents interviewed had been consulted about their children's placements, and had been invited to and had attended case reviews. Complaints about review procedures mostly centred around the venue. Parents tended to feel uncomfortable in the foster parents' home, where reviews were commonly conducted, and found it difficult to offer criticisms about the foster placement in the foster parents' presence. Some said that social workers also often failed to introduce a criticism about the foster parent which had been made to them beforehand.

Another common complaint was that parents at reviews were not invited to speak until last when all the decisions had been made already by the other people present. Hardly surprisingly, parents' perception of themselves as 'rubber stamps' tended to increase the greater the number of people present at the review and the more people who were unfamiliar.

In sum, then, we have said that, although the term 'partnership' would seem to imply a sharing of responsibility between the parent and the SSD, there is some confusion over the degree to which each party is responsible for what. From the point of view of SSDs, the purpose of the 'partnership' is to support parents in the exercise of their responsibilities - and, concomitantly, to assume as few responsibilities as possible themselves. From the parents' perspective, SSDs are pushing back on to the parents responsibilities which properly belong to the state: for example, responsibility for truant, pregnant, drug addicted or delinquent youths. 'Partnership', from this point of view, may mean that children are accommodated near enough to home to continue to create havoc, and are returned home before parents feel able to cope. It may also mean that parents bear the brunt of the Act's 'child-centredness' and are left to deal with disgruntled siblings and all the other family frictions which can result from differential treatment of a single child.

We will conclude this chapter, as before, with a summary of the key points of the discussion, together with associated ways forward. In the next chapter, we will examine 'partnership' again, but this time from the perspective of the children being served.

SUMMARY

Key points

1. Parents tend to believe that SSDs are responsible for remedying safety hazards in the home.

2. Children who are the focus of the social worker's attention are usually those children who have already been identified as in need of protection. The siblings of these children - who are largely being ignored, according to their parents - are children in need of preventive service. From the parents' perspective, social workers are too concerned with the welfare of a single child and not sufficiently concerned with the welfare of the family as a whole: that is, they are concerned with protection at the expense of family support.

3. Some parents with disabled children, while grateful for the help they were receiving, felt that this help should be extended to their other children, whose 'normal' lives were being disrupted by their sibling's disability.

4. There is some concern that children are being returned home before parents feel ready to cope with the responsibility: in other words, that the concept of parental responsibility is being used as a means of negating social services' own responsibility.

5. A major parental concern is truancy. Parents are intensely frustrated by the seeming inability of any authority to enforce the law regarding school attendance. Parents are also reluctant to talk to teachers and tend to believe that social workers should act as intermediaries between the family and the school, the police and the school, and the special and local schools.

6. Temporary placement in a special school following difficulties in the local school is perceived by parents to do more harm than good if gains are not maintained when the child returns to the local school.

7. The difference in status between foster parents and grandparents or legal guardians seems to be giving rise to resentment. Grandparents feel that they should be afforded the same privileges and benefits as foster parents have.

8. The treats, activities and other benefits afforded to accommodated children are giving rise, in some cases, to resentment on the part of siblings.

9. Children returning home after being accommodated tend to resent the loss of the benefits they formerly enjoyed.

10. Parents tend to resent the amount of assistance provided to foster parents to care for a child, particularly when the child spends a lot of time at the natural home.

11. Parents have identified the following unmet needs:
(a) counselling services for sexual abuse victims;
(b) services for pregnant teens;
(c) services for 16-18 year old youths.

12. Many parents find it difficult to express negative opinions about foster parents in front of the foster parents in the foster parents' home. Social workers, to whom the parents have previously expressed such opinions, tend not to broach the matter either.

13. Some parents feel that they are invited to reviews simply for the purpose of acting as a 'rubber stamp'. This feeling seems to be most prevalent when they are left until last before being asked for an opinion, when there are a lot of people present at the review, and when a number of the people present are unfamiliar.

14. Many parents said that they did not have sufficient information in a variety of areas.

Ways forward

1. Greater emphasis might be placed on family centres, which the study found to be one of the services least adequately provided. Such community-based centres can not only provide multi-disciplinary social services in a more accessible and less intimidating setting: they might also act as a meeting-place for residents and as a focus for concerted community effort, facilitated by social workers, towards such goals as improved safety in the home.

2. Social workers might be encouraged to devote more effort to supporting the family as a whole rather than focusing attention upon a particular child.

3. When a disabled child is being served, more attention might be given to the affect of the disability upon the child's siblings and upon the functioning of the family as a whole.

4. While it is usually good practice to maintain family ties by finding a foster placement close to home, some parents find it very stressful to be constantly visited by their accommodated children. Social workers might be encouraged to balance the maintenance of family ties against the parent's need for at least a temporary respite, and to listen carefully to parents who say that they are not yet ready to have the child returned.

5. Support from the social worker in facilitating parent-teacher communication might go a long way towards alleviating school-related problems while, at the same time, empowering the parent and improving relationships between parent, child and school.

6. In general, protocols need to be established between social services departments and the education authority to ensure that children are not

formally excluded from school and to develop strategies to encourage attendance. Follow-up after a special placement would seem to be necessary, involving the parent, the child, the social worker, and the local school.

7. While it may be impractical to suggest that foster parents should 'adopt' a family rather than providing service to a child, social workers might encourage foster parents to include siblings in activities wherever possible and to tailor the nature of gifts so that the whole family can be included.

8. When a child ceases to be accommodated, privileges formerly enjoyed might to be phased out gradually rather than abruptly terminated.

9. If an accommodated child visits home often, money might be provided to the parent, pro rata, for the purpose of looking after the child.

10. Attention might be given to developing services for the following populations:
    (a) sexual abuse victims and their families. Sexual abuse seems to be area in which the development of treatment and education programmes should be encouraged.
    (b) pregnant teens.
    (c) 16-18 year-old youths.

11. Many parents and children find it difficult to express negative opinions about foster parents in front of the foster parents in the foster parents' home. Social workers may want to consider this aspect before deciding the venue for a review. If the foster parents' home is still considered most suitable, social workers may themselves wish to broach negative opinions about foster parents expressed to them previously by natural parents.

12. Parents and children participating in reviews should not be left until last before they are asked to express an opinion. This becomes more important if there are a lot of people present or if those present are unfamiliar to the children or parents.

13. Many parents said that they did not have sufficient information in a variety of areas. Obviously, the current reliance on social workers to provide verbal information is not working well. Information leaflets might be prepared for parents covering such common concerns as:

hyperactivity; working without losing benefits; child support; parent support groups; behaviour management; harassment by an ex-partner; personal development programmes for men; entitlements when leaving care; and so on. Social workers might then distribute the relevant leaflets (including leaflets from or about voluntary agencies and community groups), providing additional verbal explanations where necessary. This provision of written material might help to dispel parents' suspicions that information about entitlements is being deliberately withheld.

Other ways of disseminating information might also be utilised: for example, holding film shows and public meetings, or erecting information booths in public places such as shopping centres.

A multi-agency strategy needs to be developed on how information is to be produced, publicised and delivered.

5 Listening to children

In the last chapter, we looked at parents' perspectives on the services being provided by SSDs in relation to 'children in need'. In this chapter we will examine children's views, based on the data collected from personal interviews with 123 children.

It was apparent from talking with parents that those parents who had good relationships with their social workers were generally satisfied with the services provided, no matter what those services were: and, conversely, parents who did not get on well with their social workers tended to look for, and find, some focus for complaint. In short, from the parents' perspective, the 'partnership' espoused by the Act is less a partnership between the parent and the SSD than it is between the parent and the individual social worker.

This tends to be even more true in relation to children. The two related factors which emerged most clearly from conversations with children were the extent of their social isolation and their dependence upon the social worker for very basic kinds of personal contact. One child exchanged recipes with her social worker, another talked about sports with his, and neither child had anyone else with whom to discuss such ordinary topics. Children were generally very aware of the kinds of things that social workers were supposed to talk about in order to fulfil their roles: such things as drug taking, employment, progress in school, criminal or sexual activity, relationships with natural and foster parents, review and court proceedings, abusive behaviour by parents, and so forth. Social workers who discussed these things were perceived by children as merely doing their duty. Conversations about football, on the other hand, were an indication that the social worker was involved with the child on a personal level and it was this involvement that defined the quality of the 'partnership'.

From the child's point of view, partnership is being defined as a measure of the social worker's relational skills, since most social workers will approach more sensitive areas through the ordinary, comfortable topics which are of interest to the child. If we want to gain a more rounded view of the kinds of partnership which SSDs are establishing with children, we first need to be clear about what we mean by 'partnership'. It might be argued that a relationship only becomes a partnership when three basic elements are present: information, participation and satisfaction. A partner, by this definition, is one who is fully informed, who participates equally in decision-making, and who is satisfied that the mutual exchange of services is fair.

We noted in the last chapter that the most common method of dispensing information is through the social worker. Not unreasonably, perhaps, social workers tend to provide children only with the kind of information which seems to be relevant and beneficial under the circumstances: information about major life changes such as being accommodated or going home, descriptions of review or court procedures, explanations about why the child cannot go home, and so forth. In the same vein, they tend to withhold information which could potentially be damaging. For example, one very angry 16-year old girl complained that her social worker had not told her she could leave her foster home and go and live with her boyfriend if she wanted to: the boyfriend had told her that. It is difficult to blame a social worker for trying to protect a child by failing to tell her that she is legally free to live with a dubious boyfriend. On the other hand, if we are going to adopt a policy of only telling children what, in the social worker's judgement, is good for them to hear, we should not pretend that we are establishing a partnership in any real sense.

The same holds true with respect to participation. Most of the children interviewed had participated in decision-making to the extent that they had been given an opportunity to express their opinions in reviews. When asked whether people had taken notice of their opinions, it became apparent that being taken notice of, in many children's minds, meant being given what they wanted. Hence, those who had not been granted what they wanted deduced - possibly erroneously - that no-one had paid them attention. Here again, we meet with the dilemma that what a child wants, in the short-term, is not always in the child's best interests in the long-term, and it is a social worker's duty to protect the long-term interests. Indeed, a few of the older children interviewed said quite frankly that decisions to which they had objected at the time had worked out better for them in the end and, in retrospect, they were grateful for having been ignored.

Thus, we might quite reasonably argue that a child's wishes should only be taken into account when granting the wish is unlikely to result in negative consequences for the child. The child's desires can only be one factor - albeit an important factor - in a decision-making process which is controlled by someone else. However, if we are going to argue this, again we cannot pretend that we are entering into any real partnership with the child.

We might note here that the someone else who controls the decision-making process is not the parent either. We said in the last chapter that children who wish to go home are sometimes sent home despite their parents' protests, and this can be particularly problematic if the child is beyond the parents' control and constitutes a physical or psychological danger to other family members. At the other end of the spectrum, the degree to which 'voluntary' care is really voluntary has been called into question by parents who do not believe that the child would have been left at home had they not agreed to voluntary care. We might thus come to the conclusion that the real decision-making power still rests with the state. Parents' and children's views are taken into account but the final decision is made by the SSD in the context of the child's best interests and in line with current government policy.

Along with decision-making power must come responsibility. We will return to the issue of responsibility later in the chapter, but first we should explore the third partnership element - satisfaction with the services provided. Study findings showed that those children who had good relationships with their social workers appeared to be generally satisfied with services while those who had poor relationships did not. While this is hardly surprising, it might be noted that the satisfaction expressed by children who had social workers did not extend to siblings who were not being served. As discussed in the last chapter, a focus on individual children rather than on entire families often results in family friction, to the eventual detriment of the child.

With respect to unmet needs - that is, to services not being provided - the most prevalent need identified by the children interviewed was for emotional support. This need was expressed in various ways, most of the children merely saying that they wished they had someone to talk to. Some wanted the social worker to visit more often, while a number of those who had left care and were living alone wanted new friends as opposed to the friends they had had before. The adolescents leaving care had usually been provided with flats but had little subsequent contact with the social worker, poor links with family, no job or community contacts, and tenuous ties with former friends who were often involved with crime and drugs. One youth had solved the problem of unwanted former friends by allowing them the use of his flat while he himself moved back to live with his mother: a solution which, according to the mother, created enormous problems for herself and his younger siblings.

A second frequently expressed desire was for a foster home. Some of the children who wanted this did not so much want a foster home as any avenue of escape from their own homes, but others were specific about the kind of advantages that having a foster home might bring. All had siblings or friends who were being accommodated and had either been to visit them in their foster homes or had listened to their stories. One child talked about having her own room, several said that they liked their siblings' foster parents and most mentioned material advantages such as clothes, holidays and trips. Concern with material goods appeared to be relative: a matter of comparisons with what other children had or what the child had had before, while being accommodated.

As previously noted, those children who had good relationships with their social workers seemed satisfied overall with the services provided, but those who had poor relationships did not. We come here to the question of what avenues are open to parents and children to allow them to express their dissatisfaction: in short, to the matter of complaints procedures.

The vast majority of the children interviewed said that they would not know how to make a complaint, while those who purported to know all said that they would complain to their social workers. When asked what they would do if they wanted to complain *about* their social worker, a few said that they would telephone the social worker's 'boss' but most had no idea. A small minority of parents were more sophisticated, citing such methods of complaint as writing a letter or telephoning the team leader, but the majority, very clearly, had given no thought to the matter and had received no information from the SSD about it.

Questions to parents on what they might complain about revealed that grounds for complaint would include not only dissatisfaction with services being received but also demands for additional services to which they felt entitled. For example, one mother provided a list of possible reasons for complaint, including both unsatisfactory service - she was unhappy with her daughter's foster home - and non-existent service - she thought that her older, pregnant daughter should be entitled to housing *before* the baby was born. The Children Act addresses both complaints about service and representations for service, stating that every local authority shall establish a procedure for considering any representations, including any complaint, made to them by a child, a parent, a foster parent, or anyone else with a legitimate interest in the child's welfare.

The Act itself says nothing about the precise mechanics of the complaints procedure except to require the participation of an independent person. However, government regulations together with the associated guidance describe a two-stage complaints procedure which local authorities are required to implement. They are also required to 'give such publicity to their procedure for considering representations under this section as they consider appropriate'.

The 'appropriateness' of publicising a complaints procedure is subject to the same difficulties as publicising services. Managers are reluctant to publicise services for fear of creating a demand they will not be able to meet: and, in the same vein, they are reluctant to provide information about complaints procedures for fear of a deluge of minor complaints. In light of the large number of relatively trivial complaints expressed to the interviewer during the course of the study, this is a fear which is probably justified. On the other side of the coin, it was apparent that complaints about even major matters were only presently being expressed by parents sufficiently articulate, or sufficiently angry, to persist against all obstacles.

As Department of Health guidance points out, "it is not intended that all problems that arise in the day to day handling of child care services should automatically be elevated to the status of a complaint." A 'complaint' is defined in the guidance as a "written or oral expression of dissatisfaction or disquiet in relation to an individual child", but it is expected that most such expressions of disquiet can be dealt with at an informal level, without referral to the complaints procedure.

This too is probably a reasonable expectation. Most of the complaints expressed to the interviewer concerned the kinds of matters that could have been dealt with by the social worker had the relationship between the parent and the social worker been good. Parents need to feel supported and heard, if not by the social worker, then by another authority figure, such as an officer designated by the SSD to hear complaints. While it may be patronising to suggest that some complaints are more akin to cries for help than real complaints, it is nevertheless true that problems will be more readily resolved if parents perceive that they are receiving attention and support rather than being blamed. The designated officer who dispenses this attention and support will be in a position to identify those complaints which warrant referral to the formal procedure. Routine recording of the complaints received will also provide data which can be used in planning to improve service provision.

If it is accepted that the majority of complaints could probably be dealt with informally by a sympathetic designated officer, there is no reason to avoid publicising the complaints procedure. Reliance upon social workers to explain the procedure is not the best method, particularly when the relationship between the parent and the social worker is poor. Distribution of leaflets through social services area offices is not much better since the proportion of parents who actually read such leaflets is apt to be low. More effective methods might include displaying posters, sending out letters to service users, raising the issue of complaints in public meetings, discussions and reviews, and setting up groups for parents and children to give them some input into the operation of complaints procedures.

So far, then, we have said that children tend to judge the degree to which they are partners with the SSD in terms of their relationship with the individual social worker. If this relationship is good, they are generally satisfied with the services provided, accept that they are fully informed, and believe that they are participating in decisions made about them. However, social workers who are acting to protect the child's best interests may sometimes override the child's desires or withhold from the child potentially harmful information. In short, social workers adopt a paternalistic, protective stance towards children in their care.

Much the same is true with respect to parents. They too judge the degree of their partnership with the SSD on the basis of their relationship with the social worker, trusting the social worker - if the relationship is good - to keep them informed, respect their opinions, and provide them with all the services to which they are entitled. However, there are enough parents who feel that they are not fully informed, that their wishes are overriden, and that they are not receiving their entitlements to bring the whole idea of an equal partnership into question. It would appear that social workers are adopting a paternalistic stance towards parents as well, juggling the welfare of the child with the dictates of the department, and providing whatever services and information seems to them to be appropriate under the circumstances.

Few avenues of complaint are open to dissatisfied parents since complaints procedures have not been adequately publicised. Effective publication would doubtless lead to a deluge of minor complaints, especially at the beginning, but sympathetic handling would avoid the necessity of referring each complaint to a time-consuming and costly formal review.

We have arrived at the conclusion that an equal partnership with parents and children probably does not exist in practice, while partnership in the client's perception depends on the quality of the relationship established with the social worker. It might be worth our while to look more closely at the ramifications of this conclusion.

In general, social workers seem to be doing very well at establishing relationships with children. When asked with whom they would discuss a personal problem, many children chose the social worker, and even those who said that they would first discuss it with a friend selected the social worker as their second confidant. Many children did not mean by 'friend' a member of their peer group. One girl in bed and breakfast accommodation had made a friend of the woman who ran her boarding house: another had struck up a friendship with the driver of a bus she often caught; and a third was friendly with a neighbour's lodger. While there is nothing wrong with counting a bus driver as a personal friend, the value which this child placed upon her conversations between bus stops does point to the paucity of her other personal relationships. In company with many of the other children interviewed, she seemed ambivalent about her peer group. On the one hand, they were old-time acquaintances, very much physically present in the neighbourhood and not easy to avoid. On the other hand, they were often involved in crime and drugs, and any movement away from their lifestyle towards the social worker's approval meant a move away from them.

It is also interesting, in this context, to note the people with whom the children interviewed would *not* discuss a personal problem. Most would not discuss it with a parent, sibling or other relative and almost none would choose to discuss it with a teacher. We are looking at children who have progressed sufficiently to be uneasy in the company of their former peer group but whose very progress has restricted their personal contacts to occasional acquaintances and mainly to the social worker. Not surprisingly, a major fear expressed by these children was that their case would be closed and the social worker's visits would come to an end. Social workers, of course, do aim eventually to close cases and terminate relationships. It may not be too much to suggest that they are sometimes thwarted in this aim by children who invent problems, precipitate crises, or otherwise do their best to ensure that they will not be left alone in a frightening limbo, caught between their peer group's world and the social worker's world: a world just barely glimpsed in which they have not the skills to function.

In our society, we have moved away from the philosophy, so prevalent earlier in the century, of rescuing children from 'bad' environments and placing them elsewhere in order to give them a fresh start. Our philosophy now is to keep them in their environments, maintain them with their families, send them to their local schools and preserve their links with friends. While there can be no doubt that our new philosophy is an improvement over the old, it does seem that we are failing to address the problem that lay at the root of the 'rescue and fresh start' philosophy: the enormous difficulties faced by children who are trying to change themselves in an environment that remains essentially the same.

Social workers do try to change the environment, particularly within the family, and often they succeed. One 12 year-old who had been accommodated while her mother was in an alcohol rehabilitation centre said that her whole life was different now that she was no longer left alone to cope with her younger siblings. Other children also pointed to improvements: the absence of a mother's abusive partner, or a good relationship with a foster parent, or a change for the better in a parent's behaviour. Nevertheless, for many children, the environment changes only temporarily while they are being accommodated, or it does not significantly change at all.

We mentioned in the last chapter the difficulties that many children face at school. Special placements seem to work well so long as they last, but there is generally little follow-up and little communication between the special and local schools, the parent and the child. The child returns in essence to the same situation as before: an anxious and often impotent parent; a reputation among teachers for being a poor and troublesome student; and a reputation among peers for being a member of a possibly esteemed delinquent group.

Children who have previously been in trouble with the police are worse off yet. A number of children complained about police 'harassment', saying that they were automatically stopped and questioned because the police knew them and assumed that, even if they had not committed the break-in or stolen the car, they would know who had. In all probability, these stories were true enough, and it is difficult to blame police officers for trying to solve crimes by questioning likely suspects. However, the effect on children who are in this instance guiltless and who are trying moreover to escape from a delinquent peer group is a feeling of despair. They are already labelled and nothing they do, or fail to do, will make much difference.

The same holds true in other areas. Children who materially lived well while being accommodated return to their parents' poverty, see it more vividly than they did before and are helpless to change it. If they have been weaned from drugs, they often return to drug-using peers. If they have learned new ways of relating or new approaches to solving problems, they return to the old ways and the old, inadequate approaches. They are no closer to finding employment than they ever were: no closer to finding a friend or marriage partner who will support them in a different way of life: no closer to anything, in fact, but an added frustration and despair.

It is small wonder that social services departments are overloaded with well-known families, with children who return again and yet again, with *their* partners and *their* children. Research evidence has shown us that abusive or neglectful parents are not 'bad' people or 'bad' parents. Abusive behaviour need not run in families: the 'vicious cycle' can be broken: families kept together can be healed. Armed with this new knowledge, we understand now that the answer to domestic violence, to truancy, delinquency and drug abuse, is not to remove children or break up families. We have got so far, but we still do not know what the answer *is*.

Perhaps, in part, it is to look more closely at the 'rescue and fresh start' philosophy which is so alien to our present mode of thought. The proponents of this philosophy solved the problem of a 'bad' environment by removing children from it. If we think that removing children is unwise while still accepting that the environment affects the child, then surely we are obliged to try to do something about the environment: not just the family environment but *whole* environment: not just a partnership with parents, but a partnership with the community as well.

We remarked in the last chapter that the Children Act emphasises the new concept of parental responsibility, and that the purpose of an SSD's partnership with parents is to support them in the exercise of their responsibility. We also observed that this interpretation of 'partnership', in which the parent bears the bulk of the responsibility and the SSD is only the support, is leading, in some cases, to parents being given a responsibility for truant, delinquent or drug-addicted children which they do not feel able to assume. According to these parents, the nature of the SSD's support is to transfer the child to a special school placement, or to accommodate the child for a while, or to find the child

68

a drug rehabilitation programme, and then, their duty done, to return the child to the home and expect the parent to cope.

If this kind of partnership is working as badly as it seems to be, and if we are philosophically - and financially - averse to implementing a partnership where the SSD assumes more of the responsibility, it is surely time to turn our attention to a three-way partnership between the SSD, the family and the community. Better yet, we might look at a multi-faceted partnership between the family, the foster family if applicable, all the departments of the local authority, voluntary organisations, community groups, and private and public concerns, such as financial institutions.

While this is hardly a new idea, emphasis upon it as a primary focus of attention would seem to be almost revolutionary. It might even be argued that the Act itself, in focusing upon the primacy of the child and the responsibility of the parent, has had the inadvertent effect of guiding us away from environmental concerns, and even away from a social interaction model of practice, towards an approach which is more akin to the individual pathology theory. Even the requirement for agencies to work together is directed towards providing service to the child, not to promoting the kind of social change which the welfare of the child must ultimately demand.

With respect to social change, we might imagine a 'one-stop-shop', used by those who receive social assistance and those who do not, where community well-baby clinics and doctors' offices rub shoulders with job centres, education and career counselling services, police-run victim assistance programmes, play groups, children's clubs, recreational and leisure facilities, flats-to-rent billboards, charity shops, financial and legal advice bureaus, and the host of other requirements which together make up Social Services - not a department now but a way of life, a universal in our residualist era, with a church at one end, a pub at the other, and a children's playground firmly at the centre.

It may be difficult to envisage such a complex, erected at the heart of every town. However, imagination is the first step towards achievement, and we have already begun by involving our communities in the development of multi-agency family centres. Relatively speaking, these centres are receiving little attention, partly due to the familiar egg-and-chicken syndrome whereby the cost of protective services leaves too little over for the establishment of those preventive services which alone can reduce the burden on protection.

It is perhaps worth stressing here that, while services may be resources-led, they are also very dependent upon attitudes. What services do we believe should receive priority? By what means do we think they should be delivered? Do we suspect that social workers might lose status if they were removed from their specialist offices and relocated between the baby clinic and the flats-to-rent? If we are advocates of family support delivered in a community setting -

and we have given up on status anyway - we might find that there are ways of obtaining the necessary funds.

Abuse and neglect must obviously still receive priority, but it has been suggested by the Department of Health that some funds from investigation and assessment might be released into family support and treatment services. Add these to other funds made available because of the smaller number of care orders following the Children Act; add these again to the money we might save if SSDs were organised differently: and it is difficult to escape the conclusion that money is not the primary issue after all. The issue is what we believe - what we want - and how hard we are prepared to fight for what we want.

In conclusion, then, we are saying that the concept of 'partnership', while good in theory, has led in practice to an inconsistency between actions and attitudes on the part of SSDs, and the worst of both worlds for parents and children. With respect to attitudes, SSDs appear to be still paternalistic in that they take children's and parents' wishes into account only when they deem it wise. Conversely, with respect to actions, they allocate to parents more responsibility than the parents are able to assume, and they expect children to maintain change in an environment that remains essentially the same.

As before, we will end the chapter with a summary of major points and recommendations. In the next chapter, we will look at the roles played by other agencies in providing service, and at the relationships between these agencies and SSDs.

Summary of major findings and recommendations

Findings

1. Social workers tend to provide children only with the kind of information which seems to be relevant and beneficial under the circumstances. In the same vein, they tend to withhold information which could potentially be damaging.

2. Parents' and children's views are taken into account but the final decision is made by the SSD in the context of the child's best interests and in line with current government policy.

3. Those children who had good relationships with their social workers appeared to be generally satisfied with the services and information provided while those who had poor relationships did not.

4.	The two related factors which emerged most clearly from conversations with children were the extent of their social isolation and their dependence upon the social worker for very basic kinds of personal contact: that is, for emotional support.

5.	Some children feared that their cases would be closed, and there is evidence to suggest that a few were taking steps to precipitate crises so that the social worker would continue to visit.

5.	Adolescents leaving care had usually been provided with flats but had little subsequent contact with the social worker, poor links with family, no job or community contacts, and tenuous ties with former friends who were often involved with crime and drugs.

6.	It would appear that we have repudiated the 'rescue and fresh start' philosophy while ignoring the problem that this philosophy was trying to solve: the difficulties faced by children who are trying to change themselves in an environment that remains the same.

7.	Children found particular difficulty in returning to the local school, to their former peer group, to their parents' poverty and, in many cases, to harassment by the police.

8.	The vast majority of children and parents did not know how to make a complaint. Of those who purported to know, most said that they would complain to their social worker.

9.	Some of the relatively trivial complaints made by parents seemed to be founded on a need for support which they did not get from their social worker. Thus, if the complaints procedure were effectively publicised, the majority of the complaints received could probably be resolved without recourse to formal review.

Associated recommendations

1.	Complaints procedures should be publicised. Reliance on social workers and on leaflets distributed through area offices is probably unwise. More effective methods of publication might include displaying posters, sending out letters to service users, raising the issue of complaints in public meetings, discussions and reviews, and setting up groups for parents and

71

children to give them some input into the operation of complaints procedures.

2.   The second recommendation encompasses the first seven findings and simply reiterates the necessity for a primary focus on community family centres. No true partnership can exist between children and parents and SSDs until some effort is made to facilitate community input into environmental change. Reorganisation of SSDs must include the relocation of social workers, together with staff from other authority departments, back into the heart of the community, so that universal social welfare becomes an integral part of ordinary community life.

6 Inter-agency working

In the last two chapters, we looked at parents' and children's views on the services being provided by SSDs in relation to children in need. The needs most often voiced by parents and children were not just those which could be met by SSDs. Rather, they included services provided by other statutory agencies, such as health, education and housing, and needs which could best be filled by voluntary or community groups.

One point to emerge very clearly was that parents often expected the social worker to obtain services from other agencies on their behalf. It was considered the social worker's responsibility, for example, to see that they were suitably housed, or to provide information on a medical condition, or to liaise with the school about such things as transfers or suspensions. Parents were usually quite clear about the functions of other people and organisations - the school was the school, the health visitor dealt with health - but the social worker was cast in a catch-all role. Social workers who could not dispense legal advice, or negotiate with the probation officer or obtain benefits from social security were often considered to be unhelpful if not incompetent.

While social workers may not feel that they are *responsible* for obtaining services from other agencies, many do quite willingly assume a liaison or advocacy role. In some cases, the role of intermediary is thrust upon them since it is often they who must co-ordinate a response to a delicate situation by gathering information from staff in other authorities and merging the various perspectives to gain an overall view. In light of the fact that social workers tend to work in practice at the interface between various agencies - and tend to be blamed by parents when things go wrong - it is worth spending a little time exploring the difficulties most commonly encountered.

Study findings showed that, of seven statutory agencies - education, health, police, probation, youth, DSS and housing - social workers found most difficulty working with the education authority. This finding is probably not so negative as it might appear, since a high level of contact between agencies is almost bound to result in a greater number of problems as well as greater success in co-operative endeavours. Social workers do a great deal of work with education:

conversely, they have little contact with youth services and have consequently encountered fewer difficulties.

Nevertheless, many social workers did feel that relationships with schools had deteriorated recently. The reason given was that schools have become so performance orientated that they are less tolerant than they used to be of children who have particular needs. Schools want 'good' children, and are more likely to exclude 'troublesome' children than to try and work with the family to resolve the problem. Moreover, these 'troublesome' children are often children who are labelled as 'troublesome' merely because their teachers know that they are being accommodated by the local authority. Schools are being accused of scapegoating, in short: an allegation supported by children who said that they could not succeed in school because they were labelled automatically as 'bad'.

Social workers also suggested that it is not only parents who expect the social worker to act as a 'cure-all'. School authorities seem to believe that, if a child has a social worker, then that child's problems belong to the social worker and not to school, even if the problem is encountered in the school environment: bullying, for example. Truancy was cited as another area in which teachers try to 'pass the buck' to social services. Several social workers remarked that teachers seem to expect them to make the parents force the child to come to school. Hence, if the child does not arrive, it is the social worker's fault for failing to manage the situation properly, and nothing to do with the school.

On the other side of the coin, some social workers complained that the buck was not passed fast enough: in other words, that schools are failing to make referrals until the situation has become extreme. One reason suggested for this is that education professionals do not want to appear as 'villains' in the eyes of parents. They want something done about a particular child but they do not want to be seen as the instigators of social work intervention, nor do they want to be seen to be involved in an intervention that is under way. In the same vein, a number of social workers reported problems with teachers attempting to make off-the-record referrals, not turning up to case conferences, or refusing to give evidence in court.

This is obviously a one-sided view of the situation since school authorities did not have the opportunity, during the study, to respond to the allegations. Had they been able to respond, they would doubtless have said that they do not scapegoat children, they do not pass any buck, and they make referrals at whatever problem stage they consider to be appropriate in the individual case. The likely truth of the matter is that children are scapegoated sometimes, the buck is passed sometimes, referrals are made too late sometimes; and, at other times, none of these things occur.

Whether they occur or not depends on the individual people involved and, most importantly, on the relationship between the particular education authority and the social services department. At an informal level, this relationship will also depend on the individuals concerned - interagency co-operation comes down to people, after all - but, at a more formal level, it will depend on the policies established and the protocols agreed. We will come back to policy and protocol later in the chapter. First, let us look at what social workers had to say about their relationships with health, housing, social security and the police.

Relationships with the health authority were deemed to be generally good, although the same reluctance to make referrals, for the same reason, was attributed to health personnel as to teachers: they wanted the child's needs met but they did not want to be seen by the parents to be involved.

With respect to the housing department, the main problem seemed to be lack of housing stock: too few houses to meet the needs of children and their families, and particularly the needs of children leaving care. Social workers felt that housing officials were failing to fulfil their obligations to this category of children: housing managers, on the other hand, felt that social workers were to blame in that they seemed reluctant to refer children leaving care to the housing department. Again, there is probably truth in both allegations. Social workers readily admit that their assessments of need are often resources-led: they may not assess a child as needing a service if the service is not to be had. Hence, it is quite likely that some social workers do fail do refer children leaving care to the housing department; and it is just as likely that some of the children referred are failing to be served because of the housing shortage. Be that as it may, social workers are alleging that housing departments are inflexible in the way that they apply the rules; housing managers are alleging that it is social workers who are obstructing service provision by failing to make referrals; and the people who are suffering most are the children who are not obtaining flats.

The same kind of scenario exists with respect to the department of social security. Social workers seem to feel that social security workers are frequently judgemental and insensitive, and lack awareness of the material hardship being experienced by clients. A number of social workers remarked with some heat that more social security workers should get out of their offices and see for themselves the appalling conditions in which poor families are obliged to live. Social security workers were accused of adopting hostile and negative attitudes towards clients living in poverty, and of labelling them as the 'undeserving' poor. The concern was also raised that incorrect advice had been given to clients regarding entitlements and benefits.

With respect to the police, social workers generally seem to be experiencing two main problems. The first is that some police officers tend to be patronising, insensitive and judgemental; and the second is that the differing aims and methods of the police and social services are giving rise to difficulties. Although the unfortunate attitude of some police officers is by no means common to all police officers, social workers do seem to feel that the police can be obstructive, punitive and inflexible at times, showing little sensitivity to the needs of children and their families, and little consideration towards social workers. One example of this lack of consideration is the procedure often followed when young people need the presence of an appropriate adult at a police station. Social workers complain that police often ring them before trying the parent, expect them to turn up as required, for as long as is required, at any time of the day or night, and keep them hanging around when they do attend.

The different agendas of the police and social services may also be an issue. In the joint investigation of suspected child abuse, the police officer's role is to assess criminal responsibility, while the social worker's role is to protect the child. These different and sometimes conflicting aims are difficult to reconcile in interviews where the social worker wants to assess risk while the police officer wants details of the abusive situation. However, on the other side of the coin, social workers do seem to feel that joint investigations are less traumatic for the child than separate investigations; and indeed, that much joint work with the police is in general positive and productive.

In sum, then, while much of the contact between SSDs and other agencies is positive, conflicts are arising due to two main factors: lack of communication and understanding; and limited resources. Scarce resources tend to engender conflict as individual agencies may try to save money by passing the responsibility for clients to someone else. Most of the friction between agencies seems to arise over referrals and disagreements about who should take responsibility for particular clients.

Limited resources may also contribute to a lack of communication and understanding since both commodities, at a formal level at least, cannot be obtained without cost. The expense involved in holding meetings, workshops and forums, developing joint protocols and training schemes, and organising interdisciplinary teams and consultative panels will usually be considerable.

Further, many co-operative ventures will not be undertaken unless each partner believes that the other can do its share. This is particularly an issue with respect to co-operation with voluntary agencies. Study findings showed that voluntary organisations are finding it difficult to obtain the funds to carry on their normal activities, let alone to engage in development work in partnership with social services. Where development work is still being undertaken - and some counties have cut it altogether - social services are reluctant to engage in joint partnership with voluntary organisations since there is always the risk that the voluntary organisation, with no statutory responsibility, might withdraw from the project at any time.

Under the Children Act, SSDs are expected to facilitate the provision of services by the voluntary sector. In practical terms, however, this frequently entails giving the voluntary organisation the money to provide the service. Often, the money is not available: and in cases where it is available, SSDs are still reluctant to provide it for two reasons. First, given the lack of adequate monitoring and evaluation systems, it is difficult for SSDs to evaluate how effectively the money is being used. Second, some voluntary organisations have aims which may, from time to time, come into conflict with social services' own aims. An example here is that workers in some women's groups may prioritise the needs of the mother above those of the child and hence may disagree with social workers about how a case should be handled. From the perspective of these groups, social workers sometimes show a lack of understanding of the needs of clients and a lack of sensitivity regarding the organisation's methods of work.

Here again, conflict seems to be arising more because of poor communication than because of any real value issues. From a practice perspective, the consequences of failure to communicate can sometimes be disastrous: enquiries into child abuse tragedies, such as the Cleveland child sexual abuse affair, have frequently highlighted inadequacies in interagency communication and co-operation. However, it is far easier to demonstrate past failings than it is to construct an effective legal framework for future co-operation, and it is particularly difficult to enshrine such a framework in law. Under the Children Act, agencies are required to co-operate in certain areas, but the frequent use of qualifying phrases - co-operation *where appropriate* or *where possible* - means, in practice, that local authorities have a considerable amount of discretion in deciding how far their co-operation should extend. In view of this, it is worth our while to take a look at the kinds of co-operation which presently exist. If we examine current efforts in the context of some logical framework, we might be able to see what is working and what is not, and where we should go from here.

Logically, the process of interagency co-operation might be seen as comprising four sequential steps: intention to co-operate, formally translated into policies; dialogue between agencies for the purpose of implementing the policies; agreements or protocols resulting from the dialogue; and joint services provided on the basis of the agreements.

With respect to policies, we have seen already in chapter 2 that policy documents generally fail to do justice to the achievements of the departments concerned. The study found little reference in policy documents to co-operation with statutory agencies and even less to co-operation with voluntary agencies, but this does not mean that co-operation is not occurring. Indeed it is, but in an *ad hoc*, sporadic kind of fashion as individual managers feel the need.

The first step towards writing a policy is to decide what we need a policy *about*: what our goals are; what it is we need to achieve and why. It is no use, for example, for SSDs to write down in their policy documents that they intend to co-operate with the education department. Co-operation is not a goal in itself: it is an activity or tool which we can use to achieve other, more specific goals. If, as we have done in this study, we ask people what their major problem areas are, we will be able to formulate goals which probably cannot be achieved without co-operation between two or more local authority departments.

Take truancy, for example. Truancy is a major concern for parents and a bone of contention between social workers and teachers, each of whom seem to feel that it is the other's responsibility. SSDs might write down in their policy documents that they intend to address the problem of truancy. They will address it by coming together with the education department and deciding, first, what constitutes truancy and, second, what is to be done when a child is truant. Should teachers refer a truant child to social services if social services are not involved already? What steps should be taken to resolve the problem with the family before the referral is made? If truant children tend to use their freedom to involve themselves in crime or drugs, as parents claim they do, should the teacher talk with the police to see if criminal activity is a problem in this particular case? Before or after talking with the parent or the social worker? What confidentiality issues will arise? How will things be different if the truant child already has a social worker?

Co-operation with the education department, and with the police department, now has a focus: to establish a procedure to be followed whenever a child is truant so that everyone knows who is supposed to do what, when, with whom and why. We may not have solved the truancy problem but at least we will have gone some way towards reducing the ill feeling that results when teachers and social workers both feel that the other should cope and the parents are left frustrated in the middle.

We can do the same thing with other problem areas. If our policy is to ensure that children returning to a local school from being accommodated or from a special placement maintain the gains that have been made, who is responsible for monitoring the child's school attendance? The child's school performance? The child's re-involvement with a former and dubious peer group? The child's relationships at home, community links, and possible criminal activities? The child's and parents' feelings, hopes and problems? Who will co-ordinate all this? How, with whom, how often?

The first step, then, is to decide what we want to achieve and formulate a policy to that effect. The second step is to get together with everyone involved and develop a protocol which will specify responsibilities, activities, referral and communication procedures, time frames, and the specifics of information exchange. This getting together will allow the formal dialogue to merge with the informal so that the resulting protocols will not exist just between social services and education but between Jane and Harry. People will know each other. They will know who is accountable for what since they know, in any particular circumstance, what colleagues in other agencies are supposed to be doing.

When we are dealing with large, sprawling bureaucracies, personal contact becomes particularly important, as does the formulation of specific goals. It may well be unproductive, not to mention expensive, to bring together anonymous representatives from various departments to talk about something nebulous, like children in need. However, if the subject under discussion is how a certain something should be done, and the people involved in the discussion are the people who are actually going to do it, a more concrete result will likely be achieved.

Take abuse investigations, for example. Although conflicts in this area still exist, both police officers and social workers interviewed during the study expressed general satisfaction with the way that child protection teams are working. Here, there is a common policy in both departments to the effect that abuse investigations should be undertaken jointly, for the purpose of acquiring the needed information with minimum trauma to the child. Next, there is a common protocol which lays down the roles, responsibilities and duties to be undertaken by police officers and social workers respectively. Finally, there is personal contact between the members of the team. Team members know, on a personal level, who is to do what, with whom, under what circumstances and why. They know this because they have trained together, acquiring insights into each other's difficulties and goals.

There is no reason why child protection teams should not be expanded to include the teacher, who will have to deal with the abused child at school, and the doctor, who may be asked to perform a physical examination. The doctor's role may be particularly important in sexual abuse cases when it will have to be decided whether and what kind of an examination ought to be performed, who should be present with the child, whose permission will be needed, who will take charge of the physical evidence, and to whom the results will be released. Doctors who are unfamiliar with the rules of evidence and, indeed, with sexual abuse examination procedures, may well benefit from the establishment of protocols into which they have had some input. Similarly, teachers may welcome the opportunity to develop some sort of co-operative framework for meeting the abused child's needs at school.

The lesson here would seem to be that interagency co-operation works best when it is focused on specific issues, and when the agreements reached have practical implications for those involved. The Audit Commission Report, *Seen But Not Heard*, notes that progress towards an interagency strategic approach to the full range of children's services has been disappointing except where it is mandatory. Various reasons are cited for this: changing agency structures, constant changes to personnel engaged in joint negotiations, a lack of skill and resources, and each agency withdrawing to its core business and wary of joint ventures (Audit Commission, 1994).

Perhaps we might postulate another reason. An interagency strategic approach is a grand endeavour, requiring a focus on the broader picture rather than on specific issues. The broader picture can only be painted at a higher level, by administrators who will not be personally involved in the practice of whatever is agreed. We might therefore expect that progress will be disappointing, both because the focus is too general and because the negotiations are being conducted at levels removed from practice in the field.

We are arguing, in short, that interagency co-operation negotiated from the top down is not only failing to work but possibly cannot be expected to work because of the human tendency to deal most effectively with issues that are specific, personal, immediate and practical. The obvious alternative is to try to co-operate from the bottom up: that is, to paint the broad picture in little sections, allowing the workers in the field to wield the brush.

Of course, there are problems with this. A picture painted by separate artists with different and sometimes conflicting perspectives is liable to lack a coherent theme and structure. The result would not be an interagency strategic approach, so much as a patchwork of multi-agency endeavours. However, this vision of potential chaos assumes that the workers are wielding the brush unguided. If they were to be guided - if higher-level administrators assumed the task of evaluating particular solutions to specific issues to see if they could be generally applied within the context of current policy - then the patchwork might come to assume a co-ordinated colour and design.

For example, we might envision a meeting between a social worker and a housing manager who are both accusing each other of obstructionist, inflexible behaviour with respect to children leaving care. The problem, according to the manager is that the social worker makes referrals only when she believes that the manager can find the child a house. Since she is unacquainted with the ebb and flow of housing stock, she has an unfortunate tendency to refer during the ebb and fail to refer during the flow, with the result that children who might be housed are not referred, and children who are referred become frustrated with the length of time they have to wait. After the recriminations have been dealt with, the manager and the social worker both agree that *all* children leaving care will be referred if they can be identified as needing to be housed. In other words, the social worker will alter her approach, from a resources-led assessment to an assessment based on needs. In return, the housing manager will provide the social worker with an ongoing update of available housing stock so that the social worker can pass on accurate information to the child.

We have here the tentative beginnings of two things: first, an information exchange between housing and social services, which might be nurtured until it grows into a system; and, second, a protocol for children leaving care. Children leaving care are usually in need of other things besides accommodation: employment, or at least job training, community links, help with budgeting and other living skills, recreational activities, and so forth. These services cannot be provided without the co-operation of a number of different agencies, all of whom might make their separate arrangements with social services about what is to be provided, how, at what stage, by whom, and on the basis of what criteria the child is to be identified as needing to be served.

These separate agreements, submitted to higher administrative levels and modified as needed, might then be moulded into an interagency protocol for children leaving care. Moreover, a somewhat different approach has been taken to the very difficult problem of defining and identifying children in need. Perhaps all children leaving care should be defined as children in need, but not all children leaving care are in need of housing. Under the Act, children are deemed to be 'in need' if they require local authority services to achieve or maintain a reasonable standard of health or development. This nebulous population of potentially needy children may be more narrowly defined if we ask what specific service it is that they require. From the housing department's perspective, children are only defined as being in need if they or their families require accommodation: and such children are readily identified on the basis of a referral from a social worker.

From the social worker's perspective as well, children in need are not children who require service in the abstract. Rather, they are children who require a specific service, assessed on the basis of specific criteria. Hence, a child in need of a house is a child 'in need' because he is homeless, or living in bed and breakfast accommodation, or living in substandard housing, or he has just come out of care.

Of course, we are not pretending that we can arrive at a definition of children in need by a process of addition. We cannot come up with a list of criteria to decide when a child needs a specific service, and add up all the lists in order to generate an exhaustive array of criteria which will cover any child who could possibly be in need. However, even if we cannot, in the abstract, use our exhaustive array as a definition of what we mean by a child in need, we may be able to use some part of this array as a basis for an interagency working protocol.

In sum, then, we have found that social workers have most contacts with the health and education departments and have reasonably good working relationships with these departments despite the problems noted. There are fewer contacts with the police, probation and housing, and fewer still with youth services and social security. Not surprisingly, most problems arise where there are most contacts, and these problems have mostly to do with referrals, lack of understanding of each other's views, and disagreements over who should take responsibility for particular clients.

We have argued that the solution to these problems lies in the establishment of specific protocols: agreements between agencies about who is responsible for doing what, for whom, how, when, why, and in what particular time-frame. Such protocols are generally lacking, and we have suggested here that the top-down approach might be productively complemented by working from the bottom up. Grass roots efforts between individuals or groups will not only facilitate personal contact but will allow an exchange of values, goals and methods which will hopefully lead to an increased appreciation of each other's roles.

A final point which needs to be taken into account is the documentation and dissemination of interagency protocols once they are established. SSDs are already involved with other agencies in numerous different projects, from working multi-disciplinary teams to consultative panels to joint assessments. However, social workers who are not directly engaged in these endeavours have little general knowledge about the kinds of agreements which exist between their own and other agencies; and the same holds true for workers in other organizations and departments, even those who sit on interagency committees. Moreover, there would seem to exist no clear written record of all the agreements which social services have reached with other agencies. In light of this, we might suggest that documentation and dissemination should be regarded as an integral part of every protocol: documentation as an aspect of policy development, and dissemination as a part of training.

As before, we will conclude this chapter with a summary of the key points, along with recommendations as to how we might move forward. In the next chapter, we will explore the implications for practice of cultural issues.

Key points

1. Logically, the process of interagency co-operation might be seen as comprising four sequential steps: intention to co-operate, formally translated into policies; dialogue between agencies for the purpose of implementing the policies; agreements or protocols resulting from the dialogue; and joint services provided on the basis of the agreements.

2. Current policy documents contain little reference to co-operation with other statutory agencies and even less to co-operation with voluntary organisations. However, this does not mean that dialogue, agreements in

some areas and some co-operation in service provision have failed to occur.

3.   The standard of documentation of agreements reached seems generally to be poor.   In the same vein, social workers are rarely aware of the existence of protocols with which they have not been personally involved. The result of poor documentation and dissemination is some confusion over what has been agreed with whom and what the practice implications are.

4.   Social services and education are the authorities most likely to be involved in interagency dialogue, closely followed by health. The police and probation services are involved to a lesser extent, while the housing authority, the Department of Social Security and youth services are least involved. Not surprisingly, most conflict tends to be encountered where there is most contact.

5.   Most social services departments have taken steps to facilitate the provision of services by voluntary organisations. The main way in which voluntary agencies are assisted is through the funding of selected voluntary groups, either by means of direct grants or by partnership in providing service. Often, funding is not available: and in cases where it is available, SSDs may be reluctant to provide it for two reasons. First, given the lack of adequate monitoring and evaluation systems, it is difficult for SSDs to evaluate how effectively the money is being used. Second, some voluntary organisations have aims which may, from time to time, come into conflict with social services' own aims. In the same vein, social services are reluctant to engage in joint partnership with voluntary organisations since there is always the risk that the voluntary organisation, lacking funding and with no statutory responsibility, might withdraw from the project at any time.

6.   The conflicts being encountered generally have to do with referrals, lack of understanding of each other's roles, and disagreements over who should take responsibility for particular clients. The scarcity of resources tends to promote conflict since agencies are anxious to pass responsibility for clients to someone else.

7.   Although a number of separate agreements have been reached, the Audit Commission Report *Seen But Not Heard* notes that progress towards an interagency strategic approach has been disappointing.   In short,

interagency co-operation negotiated from the top down is not proving particularly successful. We might postulate that this is occurring both because the focus of the discussions tends to be too general and because the negotiations are being conducted at levels removed from practice in the field.

8.   Statutory and voluntary agencies are providing some joint services with social services departments. These services range from working multi-disciplinary teams to consultative panels to joint assessments. The majority of joint services, like the majority of agreements, exist between social services departments, health and education, while housing and probation are only marginally involved, and youth services and the Department of Social Security are involved least often.

9.   Local authorities remain the major providers of children's services although some do subcontract to voluntary agencies. In only a few cases are private companies used, although it has been noted by the Department of Health that the trend is towards a more pragmatic used of a mixed economy of care. In light of this trend, the development of some framework for co-operation between agencies assumes a new importance.

Ways forward

1.   More attention may need to be paid to joint work with the police and probation services, and with youth and social security departments - all organisations with whom few protocols have been established.

2.   It is suggested that the top-down approach to establishing joint agreements might be productively complemented by working from the bottom up. Grass roots efforts between individuals or groups will not only facilitate personal contact but will allow an exchange of values, goals and methods which will hopefully lead to an increased appreciation of each other's roles.

3.   Grass roots agreements might be submitted to administrators who would assume the task of evaluating particular solutions to specific issues to see if they could be generally applied within the context of current policy. Working protocols might then be developed through a synthesis of such agreements: and strategies might emerge from a synthesis of protocols.

4. Documentation and dissemination should be regarded as an integral part of every protocol. With respect to social workers and staff from other agencies whose practice will be directly affected by the protocol, it might be expected that dissemination will be achieved through joint training. However, other staff will also need to be informed. Complete and accurate documentation of the protocol is particularly essential if separate agreements are to be used as stepping stones to coherent, overall strategies.

7 Cultural concerns

In the preceding chapters, we have discussed a number of matters which are particularly relevant in the context of cultural concerns. The first is the fact that policy documents generally do not do justice to the achievements of departments and provide little specific guidance as to how their work might be improved.

The Children Act places a duty upon local authorities to take account of a child's religious persuasion, racial origin and cultural and linguistic background when considering the provision of services: and most policy documents do indeed state that these things will be taken into account. However, that is usually as far as it goes. Very rarely are cultural concerns written into policy in the form of goals, and even less often are there specified procedures through which the goals might be achieved.

For example, our goal with respect to culture is not to take a child's racial origin into account. Taking something into account is an activity, not a goal, and the reason we are undertaking this particular activity is presumably to ensure that every child has the opportunity to recognise and nurture his or her specific cultural identity. We are saying, in other words, that we do not wish the United Kingdom to become a melting pot in which the cultures of minority groups are submerged and assimilated into the majority British culture. Rather, our goal is to establish a mosaic where different cultures are respected and preserved and enabled to live together as a harmonic whole.

It might be worth pointing out that this is a very difficult goal for a country with the colonial history of Britain. Historically, as a nation, we have taken pride in Empire, and the way we built our Empire was to pursue a deliberate policy of assimilation: to impose upon other cultures our language, our religion, and our political and economic systems, while persuading ourselves that we were inherently superior and had a moral duty to teach our ways to our subject, backward peoples. In general, we persuaded ourselves very effectively, and it would be foolish to assume that we can easily shrug off four hundred years of history in order to pursue a radically different cultural policy. There are still British people who do not want to see the mosques rise beside the churches or the yams appear next to the potatoes, or the black faces mingle with the white:

and some of these may well be workers in various local authority departments responsible for serving children in need.

Nevertheless, let us assume that our overall goal is to facilitate the creation of a cultural mosaic in the United Kingdom. If this is the case, then our first step with respect to child and family service departments is to write in our policy documents that we intend to move towards this goal by providing each child with the opportunity to assume his or her own cultural identity. There are three reasons why doing this may create some difficulty. First, managers may argue that the department as a whole is committed to providing services on the basis of choice, bearing in mind ethnic issues, and a separate policy is therefore not required in the area of child and family services. This argument assumes a level of intra-departmental co-ordination and communication which may indeed exist in some departments. However, as a basis for standard practice, such an assumption is possibly unwise.

The second reason lies in the wording of the goal itself. The trouble with stating a goal in the first place is that performance can then be judged on the degree to which the goal has been achieved: and the more specific the goal, the easier it is to make the judgement. If we are sufficiently vague - saying, for example, that we will take the child's racial origin into account - it will be difficult to evaluate the extent to which we have succeeded. If we are a little more precise, saying that we will enable children to maintain their cultural identities, it may be pointed out that we failed in the case of a Pakistani child whose English foster parents did not take him to a mosque.

Things grow even worse when we come to specify the procedures through which we will attain our goals. We might believe, for example, that children can only really maintain their cultural identities if they are placed with foster or adoptive parents from the same cultural background as themselves. If we specify in our procedures manuals that children and parents will be ethnically matched, we are liable to run into trouble when we find that there are not enough Hindu or Korean or Nigerian parents to go around. Similarly, we might specify that the social worker will always be able to speak the first language of the child, or that play group equipment will be ethnically sensitive, or that leaflets will be printed in the language of the service user, or that carers will prepare ethnically appropriate food. Since managers are not in a position to guarantee any of these things, it is hardly surprising that they are reluctant to commit themselves in writing to services which they are unlikely to be able to provide and on the basis of which their performance may be judged.

Nevertheless, avoidance is hardly the route to goal achievement. If we really want to recruit more Nigerian foster parents, we must first say that we do, and then we must make a planned, coherent effort to establish relationships with the appropriate communities so that we can find and train - and allow ourselves to be trained by - Nigerian people. Similarly, if we want more Nigerian social workers, we must co-operate with communities and with institutions of higher education to attract and train them. If we want leaflets printed in a foreign language, we must approach communities to find translators, and negotiate with other agencies who might be prepared to share the service and the cost.

There are several ways to reduce the cost of providing culturally appropriate services. First, as we have already noted, co-operative endeavours between agencies might allow for joint translation services and the joint production of multi-lingual materials such as forms, pamphlets, manuals and the like. Such endeavors might also assist SSDs in complying with the duty laid down in the Act to publish information not only about their own services but also, where appropriate, about the services of other statutory and voluntary agencies.

Second, efforts might be made to augment or replicate the joint - and therefore more cost-effective - training schemes which are already in operation in some areas. Cultural issues could then be explored from the different perspectives of professionals who are providing different though related services to vulnerable children and their families. Since such schemes are already in operation in the area of child protection, it would seem a not illogical step to take them forward into other areas of child care practice. Workers in various fields have often remarked that joint training leads to increased understanding of the roles and responsibilities of other agencies and enhanced communication and working relationships.

Nevertheless, no-one can deny that culturally-appropriate services are expensive to provide. They are relatively more expensive if the ethnic population they are meant to serve is small: and this brings us to the third reason for the reluctance of managers to be specific about culturally-related goals. If only one per cent of the population served by a particular SSD speak Welsh as a first language, for example, is it worth providing a totally bilingual service? Taking into account the fact that most of these Welsh speakers will also speak English, is it worth going to the expense of providing Welsh lessons to social workers, printing information in Welsh and English, hiring translators, and making special efforts to recruit Welsh-speaking foster parents and carers? On the opposite side of the coin, we should not forget that the small numbers of Welsh speakers who do not speak English are liable to include the most vulnerable members of the population: the elderly, the very young, those with learning difficulties, the housebound, and people living in isolated areas. Moreover, even those who do speak English as a second language may face acute difficulties when asked to communicate private and emotional concerns in a language not their own. Taking this into account, can we justify failing to provide full service in Welsh?

Study findings show that SSDs serving areas in which there is a high proportion of Welsh speakers among the general population tend to provide bilingual service and have policies to that effect. Conversely, where there is only a small proportion of Welsh speakers among the general population, bilingual service is not routinely provided, and policies specifically relating to the Welsh culture and language do not exist. Moreover, managers feel that there is no reason for such policies to exist *because* of the small numbers of clients to whom they would practically apply.

There are three issues here. First, managers who see no reason to institute policies do try to provide services in Welsh where necessary, on a reactive rather than a routine basis. In other words, there *is* a policy: an unwritten, informal policy to the effect that a response should be made in the first language of the client wherever possible. Such an informal policy allows managers to comply with general departmental policy about taking the child's cultural background into account while avoiding specific, written commitments which they may not be able to fulfil. Moreover, providing a service only on request has the effect of reducing the demand for service since the demand will usually remain low when the responsibility for obtaining access to the service is placed upon the service user. When the service is provided routinely in a convenient and non-stigmatising manner, not only does the demand increase among existing users but new approaches are made by those who have previously considered social work services to be too far removed from their own experience to be of benefit. Hence, a lack of formal policy due to a small client population tends to make the population even smaller: hardly a prescription for prevention.

There are other limitations to informal policies which we have mentioned before in previous chapters but which will bear repeating here. Lack of a formal policy may mean that service will be discontinued or curtailed when present staff move on. It may mean that parameters of service provision are unclear and are not consistent throughout the department: it may also mean that some staff will perceive culturally-oriented services as unimportant because they have not been given the weight of formal expression. It will almost certainly mean that monitoring and evaluation procedures will be lacking since it is not possible to evaluate the degree of achievement of a goal which has never been formally expressed.

We are saying, then, that policies with respect to ethnic groups should be formulated no matter how small the group in relation to the general population. These policies need not say that service *will* be provided: if there is only occasionally a Hindu child in a play group, say, it may not be possible to guarantee that one of the group leaders will speak Hindi and there will be books in Hindi and culturally-appropriate toys. Nor may it be possible to guarantee that the duty social worker will always speak Welsh - or French or Gujarati -

or that the required number of Nigerian foster parents will be found. However, the policy might stipulate that steps will be taken to recruit foster parents, social workers and carers with requisite cultural backgrounds, or that efforts will be made to provide appropriate toys. Certainly, the policy might specify what is to be done in the event that culturally-appropriate service cannot immediately be provided: if an investigation needs to be conducted, for example, and the social worker who would normally be appointed does not speak the family's language. Interim evaluation could then be conducted on the basis of what steps have been taken, rather than on what has been accomplished - although the appropriate steps are obviously expected to lead to achievement in the end.

With respect to Wales, study findings show that steps have been taken to make provision for Welsh-speaking clients and that difficulties have been encountered. For example, local authorities who encourage job applications from Welsh speakers may be accused of discriminatory employment practices and hence of racism by extremist anti-nationalist groups who do not want to see the speaking of Welsh encouraged in Wales. It is easy to envision the same accusations being levelled by white groups against authorities who actively seek to recruit non-white social workers, foster parents and carers. Racial issues are always problematic because they are fuelled by intense emotions and are rarely amenable to resolution through negotiation. It is therefore difficult to suggest solutions, except to learn from others who have trodden the same tension-ridden path: police administrators, for example, and the non-white police officers employed by them, who may have developed successful strategies to cope with harassment and rejection, both by the white majority and by their own particular cultural groups.

Another possible problem is the marginalisation of non-white staff. If we have succeeded in recruiting one Hindu social worker, it might seem entirely reasonable to assign all Hindu clients to him or her. We might even go so far as to assign all black clients to black social workers, on the assumption that black will be better understood by black, regardless of the differences in actual cultural background: a Ghanaian client with a Jamaican social worker, for example. The result of this kind of painting by numbers may well be a redrawing, in our own offices, of the very racial lines we intended to eliminate, with the non-white social workers and their non-white clients pushed to the fringe of our white-white majority activities.

A related problem is compartmentalisation which tends to occur if efforts are focused, as they have been, on specific aspects of the department's work, such as adoption and fostering, or services for the under-fives. We do not really want to develop policies on racial issues with respect to one particular client population: we want policies which can be more generally applied. Perhaps we do not even want to develop policies on racial issues: we may want policies instead which are related to the broader area of equal opportunities. We need to think these things through very carefully, making sure that we do not seize upon solutions without a thorough understanding of the kinds of problems that these solutions might themselves engender.

So far, we have been talking about developing policies related to cultural issues and specifying the procedures necessary to achieve our goals. Policies are a reflection of the philosophies of the policy makers in the context of limited resources. However, they must also reflect the needs of the service users, and these needs cannot be ascertained until demographic data are available. Study findings show that many departments have used census data to obtain information about the ethnic composition of their general populations. Data on language or ethnicity with respect to *client* populations are far more rare, and no data at all are available on religious affiliation. In short, it appears that SSDs possess those data which are available from census returns but have generally not collected any additional data.

It is hardly necessary to point to the difficulties of providing adequate service to clients about whom little is known, and most managers are quite aware of the limitations of census data. One reason for the lack of any concerted effort to collect additional information may lie in the nature of ethnic monitoring itself. Attitudes towards it range from the perception that it is unimportant to the view that asking about the ethnic origin of clients is in itself a racist act. We might argue that asking about ethnic origin is only a racist act in the kind of melting-pot culture where British is best and affiliation with any other culture is better swept under the rug. In the mosaic culture we have said we want to develop, people from ethnic minority groups will presumably be proud of their heritage and eager to share with others who they are, how they live and what they want. Nevertheless, monitoring race effectively is a problem experienced nationally: and we might see in that an indicator of how far we have to go in establishing our cultural mosaic.

However, reluctance to ask clients about their ethnic origin is not the only reason why demographic data have rarely been collected. Another reason lies in the general failure to incorporate monitoring, evaluation, and information systems into departmental planning. Study findings show that those departments which have established formal monitoring procedures are also those with the clearest demographic pictures. In other words, as would be expected, departments find it easier to create community profiles if they have existing information and technology sections, together with staff experienced in the collection, collation and utilisation of data.

It might be worth noting here that the kind of data needed for sensitive planning cannot be obtained by merely counting heads. What is required is a needs assessment *from the perspective of the service user*, including not only quantitative but also qualitative data. While so obvious a point may seem unworthy of mention, quantitative data do tend to possess an aura of authority which qualitative data lack. They are also easier to collect, easier to process and, when properly presented, easier to understand. Thus, there is a real danger that the limitations inherent in numbers will be forgotten and policy will be formulated on the basis of information which is arithmetically correct but misleading in human terms.

The general lack of monitoring systems, together with the resulting dearth of information, are ascribed by managers to lack of time and resources. This again would seem to be an area in which co-operation between agencies might be employed to great advantage. A relatively small contribution from each in terms of funding, personnel and expertise could provide an information system, or at least a database, to be used for the benefit of all. In addition, the negotiations involved in such an enterprise may form a framework for the establishment of other databases, such as child protection registers. Such negotiations might include discussion about what data are to be collected, how, by whom and when, who is to have access to what under what circumstances, how the data are to be stored, and how access is to be controlled.

If only we can manage to collect the requisite data about our client population, we can formulate policies based on their needs and our philosophies, and we can establish procedures designed to meet our goals. Hopefully, both front-line social workers and client groups will have been involved in policy formulation and will be involved in monitoring goal achievement. Nevertheless, the next step is to provide training to social workers so that they will know what policies are being implemented and what procedures have been selected. All of the social workers interviewed during the study had theoretically been provided with training around cultural issues, and all knew of the existence of policy to the effect that the child's cultural background must be taken into account when providing services. However, less than half were aware of the guidance which had purportedly been given around specific issues, and less than a quarter remembered being given training.

Training which is not recalled can hardly be said to have been effective: and much of the problem appears to lie in the attitudes of social workers, harassed in practice, to policy, guidance and training presented in theory. When there is no choice of foster placement, for example, it is not particularly useful to be told that one should try to provide an ethnic match for every child. Training exercises seem not to take into account the constraints and frustrations which practically exist in the field with the result that social workers pay them little attention and forget about them quickly when they are over.

The difficulty here, as we have said before, is that there seems to be little in the way of concrete policies and procedures for social workers to be trained *in*.

No-one has said, for example: we know there is a dearth of Hindu foster parents. Here is what we propose to do about it, and here is what *you* should do meanwhile. Or: we know that you have difficulty finding placements for children from travelling families. Such children have particular educational needs as well as social and cultural needs, and are often discriminated against by other statutory agency workers as well as by wider society. We are consulting with other agencies to find solutions and here is what you do until our negotiations are concluded. Failing specific policies which take into account interagency relationships and resource constraints as well as cultural issues, it is difficult to suggest ways in which training might be made more relevant.

One specific kind of training which could be relevant is training in a foreign language. Social workers in Wales are encouraged to learn Welsh and generally feel that a greater knowledge of the language assists them in their work. However, some would argue that the quality of Welsh spoken by those who have only recently learned it is inadequate to communicate effectively with clients and certainly falls short of the standard required to conduct an investigation or interview a child. Additionally, there is the question of whether Welsh will be learned in the department's or in the social worker's time. Managers tend to feel that staff numbers are insufficient to permit time off for lessons. Social workers feel, conversely, that it is unrealistic of management to expect them to study before work or during breaks, especially in light of the fact that they frequently have no breaks due to pressure of work.

In any case, learning Welsh while working in Wales may well be a different proposition to learning Twi or Gujerati, say, while working in England. If social workers are not likely to be able to speak the various languages of clients, we might perhaps do better to focus our training on some aspects of community social work: how to approach ethnic communities so that they can train *us*: how to establish positive relationships so that we can assess needs, find translators, attract foster parents and carers, understand and respect the culture, and monitor our progress towards our mutual goals.

In sum, then, we have said that policies with respect to cultural issues tend to be restricted to a bare statement that the ethnic, cultural, linguistic and religious needs of children will be taken into account when providing services. One reason for this is that managers are understandably reluctant to enshrine in writing services they are unlikely to be able to provide. Another reason is that we seem not to think in terms of formulating goals and related procedures, disseminating these through training, and monitoring our progress to see how much we have achieved.

Because we have generally not established monitoring and evaluation systems, we do not have available the information and technology structures which would enable us to construct community profiles, including needs assessment data.

Because we do not have the data, we cannot plan to provide appropriate services and the service we do provide is full of gaps. There are not enough ethnic minority social workers, foster parents, carers or translators, and our efforts to recruit them are not sufficiently planned to make them overly successful. Resource constraints are obviously an important factor, but here again we have not really organised the interagency contacts which might enable us to share the load, nor have we devised appropriate methods for getting help from the communities we are trying to serve.

The intense emotions which are often engendered by racial issues also cannot be ignored. Solutions are always hard to find, but the same problems are being encountered by other agencies and groups and, once again, it is a matter of learning from each other's errors and working and struggling together.

As usual, we will conclude this chapter with a summary of key points together with suggested ways in which we might move forward. In the last chapter, which follows, we will draw together the points we have raised in order to further examine some of the most critical issues.

Summary of key points

1. Overall, SSDs are attempting to comply with the requirements of the Children Act by formulating general policies to the effect that the ethnic, cultural, linguistic and religious needs of children will be taken into account when providing services.

2. Policies are not always written but there is no doubt that managers do consider the cultural background of the child to be a vital factor in making decisions on the services to be provided. Indeed, the recognition of the importance of culture may be so basic as to itself constitute a danger. It may appear that something so obvious does not need to be formally enshrined in words, particularly if the authority as a whole is committed to providing service on the basis of the individual needs and choices of the service user.

3. A policy will not usually exist unless policy makers perceive that there is a need for it to exist. At present, the perception that a policy is needed seems to be largely influenced by the numbers of people to whom the policy would practically apply.

4. SSDs are able to provide data on the ethnic composition of their general populations (i.e. census data) but not of their client populations. No data

at all are available with respect to religious affiliation, and religion as an issue tends to be paid scant attention.

5. Not surprisingly, SSDs which have established formal monitoring procedures are also those with the clearest demographic pictures. In other words, departments find it easier to create community profiles if they have existing information and technology sections, together with staff experienced in the collection, collation and utilisation of data.

6. Since no data on the needs of ethnic minorities are available, social workers must adopt a reactive ('on demand') rather than a proactive approach to service provision. This has the effect of reducing the demand for services since, when a service can be obtained only on special request, the demand remains low. When the service is provided routinely in a convenient and non-stigmatising manner, not only does the demand increase among existing users but new approaches are made by those who have previously considered social work services to be too far removed from their own experience to be of benefit.

7. Achieving an ethnic match for children in foster care is difficult because of a lack of ethnic minority carers. Other problems are: language, exacerbated by a lack of translators; arguments over the practicalities of language lessons, due to resource constraints; too few social workers from ethnic minority groups; lack of awareness of ethnic needs; lack of resources for ethnic minority children; and problems in working with children from travelling families, whose unique lifestyle is rarely taken into account.

8. Local authorities who encourage job applications from ethnic minority people may be accused of discriminatory employment practices and hence of racism by extremist groups.

9. Associated issues are marginalisation of non-white staff and compartmentalisation which tends to occur if efforts are focused on specific client populations or specific aspects of the department's work.

10. Social workers appear to largely disregard guidance and training which they do not perceive as relevant to their experience in the field. The difficulty here may be that concrete policies and specific procedures which take into account interagency relationships and resource constraints have generally not been formulated. Training therefore tends to revolve

around more general issues such as race awareness. Since it does not provide specific guidance on specific problems, it may not be readily recalled.

11.   Specific training in the area of language lessons is generally welcomed by social workers, although there is some controversy over whether the lessons should be taken in the department's or in the social worker's time. Another difficulty is the inadequacy of a recently acquired language for effective communication with clients over sensitive matters.

Ways forward

1.   Formal goal-oriented policies with respect to cultural issues need to be developed. Such policies should cover all populations whatever their size. Specific policies should also exist with respect to child and family services: an umbrella departmental policy is usually insufficient.

2.   Demographic mapping needs to be completed, together with the establishment of monitoring, evaluation and information systems. Needs assessment data should be collected from the perspective of potential service users.

3.   A greater effort might be made to establish relationships with ethnic minority groups so that foster and adoptive parents and volunteers will come forward, and translators can be more readily found.

4.   In this same vein, co-operative endeavours between agencies might allow for joint translation services and the joint production of multi-lingual materials. Efforts might be made to augment the joint, and therefore more cost-effective training schemes which are already in operation in some areas; and attention might be given to liaison with educational institutions and to review of employment criteria.

8 A broader perspective

Many of the problems that social welfare practitioners have encountered in operationalising need, appear to arise from the incongruity between the all-embracing spirit of the Act and current political, economic and social realities. Therefore, we will conclude this book with a broader discussion of the context of family support, and highlight key issues and dilemmas facing social welfare practitioners and agencies as a consequence of the contradiction referred to. First, however, it will be useful to briefly consider the meaning of prevention.

The meaning of prevention

The provisions concerning support for children in need and their families contained in the 1989 Act reflect the changing meaning of prevention. As we saw in chapter 1, the concept barely existed in Victorian times. Whilst the Children Act replaces the language of prevention with that of family support, for present purposes it is useful to note that Holman (1988) distinguishes seven contemporary dimensions of prevention:

(i)   preventing children being received into public or voluntary care away from their families;

(ii)   preventing children entering custodial care;

(iii)   preventing the neglect or abuse of children;

(iv)   preventing the effects of poor parenting on children;

(v)   saving children from those disadvantages in their homes and communities associated with lack of income, amenities and social experiences;

(vi)   preventing children from having to remain in care (rehabilitation);

(vii)   preventing the isolation of children in care;

Holman (1988) considers that the key to the meaning of prevention lies in its aim or purpose. Prevention may thus be regarded reactively or positively. The former conceptualisation is defensive in nature: it concerns policies and practices which prevent the unnecessary separation of children from their parents and their placement away from home in public (or voluntary) care or custody; and, if separated, from unnecessarily having to remain in care, or being stopped from maintaining physical and/or emotional links with their natural families. A positive view of prevention entails the promotion of policies and practices aimed at preventing children from failing to enjoy in their own homes, the kind of parenting, the freedom from suffering, the standards of living, and the quality of community life which is considered reasonable for children in our society.

We are clearly a long way from achieving this positive concept of prevention. Indeed, we even appear to be some way off from achieving the markedly less exacting, reactive, concept of prevention distinguished by Holman, which centres on preventing the unnecessary separation of children from their parents and their placement away from home in care.

The context of family support

Organisation of services

That progress is slow is not surprising, given that fundamental requirements for effective family support services are lacking.

Holman (1988) identifies a number of factors which are essential for the operation of prevention. These include the localisation of services into small geographical units, which would increase the capacity of social workers to help families at an early stage of their difficulties and to enlist local resources. However, on the whole, social services departments have not adopted the community or neighbourhood approach advocated by the Seebohm and Barclay Committees (see chapter 1). Rather, they have tended to pursue a reactive stance with an associated focus on child protection. This has contributed to the fact that need is defined in terms of individual pathology rather than as a matter of social justice. On the basis of latter, whole areas rather than individual families may be defined as needy.

Many commentators consider that family centres can play a pivotal role in community-oriented family support work. Despite the fact that family centres perform a wide range of valuable tasks, they do not appear to occupy the central role that seems to be necessary for effective family support work. Further, the social workers that we interviewed in our study cited family centres as one of the least adequate services provided by their departments. This is unfortunate, for the evidence suggests that small geographical units of localised services, with a key role for family centres, would make it easier to involve users in decisions about the kinds of services that are offered; they would facilitate participation by users in the actual delivery of services, and would reflect a conception of users which focuses on their strengths as well as their limitations. In short, services organised along the lines suggested would be more conducive to establishing a genuine partnership between social workers and services users.

Social polarisation

A second pre-condition for effective family support services identified by Holman (1988) entails reducing inequality and social deprivation. In chapter 1, we traced the historical process whereby the narrow concept of 'rescue and fresh start' or 'curative prevention' which characterised the Victorian system of child welfare eventually developed into the much broader spirit of proactive family support enshrined in the Children Act 1989. This more positive approach to family support can only be effectively implemented in a society which is moving towards the reduction of inequality and social deprivation. Yet, it is plain that the United Kingdom of the 1990s does not constitute such a society. There is clear evidence pointing to increasing social polarisation.

Halsey (1988) has documented this evidence. He shows that the post-war trend towards greater equality in the distribution of income and wealth came to a halt and was reversed during the 1980s. Prior to the oil crisis of 1973-74, Britain had experienced 30 years of economic prosperity with high rates of economic growth, full employment and burgeoning public sector activity. However, Halsey (1988, p.26) reports that more recent years have seen...

> declining employment, economic activity shifting out of classical towards 'high tec' or service industry, struggles with inflation, determination to move decision making out of Westminster and Whitehall into the market and the locality and policies designed to cut back the public and strengthen the private sector.

Halsey argues that a modern version of Disraeli's 'two nations' thesis has appeared in the form of a widening gap between a prosperous majority in secure and well paid employment, and a depressed minority comprising the unemployed, the old, the sick, and unsuccessful ethnic minorities. In support of

99

his thesis, Halsey presents evidence showing increasing inequalities in (a) the distribution of income and wealth and (b) the social division in housing, which have been accompanied by (c) spatial polarisation. He observes that the...

> process is one of deprived people being left in the urban priority areas as the successful move out to middle Britain. The former have decreasing wealth, health services, income, investment, and amenity: the latter have rising affluence, opportunity, power and advantage: in one ugly word - polarisation.

A British underclass?

Of late, there has been much debate about whether an underclass is emerging in Britain. Murray (1990) has advanced a controversial conception of this social stratum. The author discerns a growing underclass which is partly defined by poverty, but more particularly by undesirable behaviour such as drug-taking, crime, illegitimacy, drop-out from the labour force, truancy from school, and casual violence. Thus, Murray appears to reinvoke the distinction between 'deserving' and 'undeserving' poor which underpinned the Poor Law in the Victorian era.

Others have vigorously disputed Murray's particular conception of an underclass. For Field (1990), the underclass consists of three groups: the retired, frail, elderly; single parents, and the long-term unemployed. While Murray holds that a distinction should be made between low income *per se* and poverty which results from anti-social and self-defeating behaviour, Field is concerned with reducing inequalities in income and wealth. Brown (1990) takes issue with Murray's view that single unmarried mothers represent a problematic group, arguing that, on average, divorced mothers spend longer on benefit than unmarried mothers; and, that never-married mothers remain lone parents for a shorter average period than divorced mothers. Walker (1990) contends that Murray's notion of the underclass 'blames the victim', which serves to divert attention from the real problem: the mechanisms by which resources are distributed. Finally, Deakin (1990, pp. 64-65) accuses Murray of advocating... 'a static form of society composed of neatly docketed and differentiated small units from which the dangerous classes have been neatly excluded.'

Despite disagreement about the concept of an underclass, few doubt that inequality has increased significantly in Britain over the past fourteen years. For example, Bradshaw (1990) reports that from 1979 to 1987 the share of final income of the bottom 20 per cent dropped by 11 per cent and that of the top 20 per cent increased by 11 per cent. Moreover, the increasing level of inequality in Britain is such that the current director-general of the Confederation of British

Industry, Howard Davies, has expressed concern about its impact on the social and economic well-being of the nation. In a well-publicised recent lecture to the Manchester Business School, Mr. Davies called on Government and employers to face up to the consequences of major economic upheavals that have transformed Britain into a more unequal society. Rejecting the laissez-faire approach adopted in the 1980s, he argued that significant improvements in training are required, together with radical changes to the tax and benefits system and policies to help the long-term unemployed back to work (Elliott, 1994).

Child poverty

Much has been written about the consequences of poverty, in terms of reduced social participation as well as unmet basic needs (e.g. Townsend, 1979; Bradshaw, 1990; Oppenheim, 1990). The evidence is well documented. By 1989, 11,330,000 people, or 20 per cent of the population were living on or below the standard set by Income Support; that final, means-tested, subsistence-level safety net of the welfare state (HMSO, 1992a; Oppenheim, 1993). A series of Reports in the early 1990s have illustrated the effects upon individuals denied not simply the basic currency of everyday life - a one week annual holiday, a haircut, a once-a-year visit to a Christmas pantomime for children (Bradshaw 1993) - but also food (Sinfield et al., 1991; Stewart and Stewart, 1993), clothing (Craig and Glendinning, 1990) fuel (NCH, 1993; Oldfield, 1993) and even water (McNeish, 1993).

Children figure prominently among those worse affected by the rise in poverty. Between 1979 and 1987, for instance, the proportion of children living below 50 percent of average income more than doubled from 12.2 per cent to 25.7 per cent. Over the same period, there was also a doubling of the number of children living in families dependent on supplementary benefit and on family income supplement (Bradshaw, 1990). According to Bradshaw (1990, p. 51) children have...

> ...borne the brunt of changes that have occurred in the economic conditions, demographic structure and social policies of the UK. ...There is no evidence that improvements in the living standards of the better-off have 'trickled down' to low income families with children.'

Few people are in a better position to observe the effects of increasing inequality and child poverty than social workers. While not all poor people have social workers, most people helped by social workers in the Britain of the 1990s are poor. To an extent unparalleled since 1945, the daily agenda for practitioners

101

is dominated by the consequences which prolonged and deepening penury produces in the social fabric of society and in the lives of families and individuals.

By the end of the 1980s, 90 per cent of new referrals to social workers came from social security claimants (Community Care, 1990). Over half of these were individuals and families dependent upon subsistence-level Income Support (Becker and Selburn, 1990). Two-thirds of all referrals - mostly women - were related to financial, benefit or housing problems and nearly one-third of these were to do with the system's so-called final safety net - the Social Fund (Becker, 1991). One the most extensive research projects which followed the setting up of the Fund found that as many as six out of ten clients in active contact with Social Services Departments were said to be self-referred for a Social Fund related problem (Stewart et al., 1989). The voice of those living in poverty in contemporary Britain has been authentically represented in a series of reports, including those from the Child Poverty Action Group and Barnardos. Drawn from the practicalities of daily life, the strength and hostility of claimants' feelings against a system characterised by stigma, vulnerability, humiliation, uncertainty and inconsistency, emerges as part of 'the mainstream of claimants' experience' which "cannot be marginalised as 'horror stories'" (Craig and Glendinning, 1990). The reports graphically explore and describe the effects of living in poverty: the prevalence of debt, the restrictions on diet, clothing and basic household items; and the consequent problems of ill-health, social isolation, personal depression and despair, and family stress and breakdown which financial insecurity brings (Barnardos, 1990).

It is significant in this context that, when asked what services they would like but were not receiving, the parents that we interviewed gave first priority to material goods and better housing. We also found that, although children living in poverty are 'children in need' under the terms of the Children Act: (a) social services departments in Wales could not provide data on the number of children living in poverty; (b) because of limited resources, children living in poverty were accorded lowest priority in terms of service provision, despite the desire of managers to engage in more preventive work; (c) services designed to alleviate poverty were provided inconsistently to users depending on the particular social worker involved; and (d) given present resource constraints and residualistic national policies, lead child care managers could see little hope of altering the situation.

Increasing household diversity

The backdrop of the Children Act 1989 not only includes a significant rise in child poverty, but also increasing diversity in the kinds of childhoods experienced by Britain's children. Two important factors underpinning the range of different childhoods that may be experienced in contemporary Britain are ethnic differences and the large proportion of households headed by single parents (Rapoport, Fogarty and Rapoport, 1982; Halsey, 1988; Abbot, 1989).

With regard to ethnic diversity, Halsey (1988, p. 15) reports that while the population of Britain rose from 38 million at the turn of the century to 58 million by 1986, there was, in fact, a *net* migration loss of 2.3 million. However, there were also migration gains, particularly of Jewish refugees, and far larger labour inflows from Ireland. Then, in the second half of the century, a five per cent minority emerged from international labour migration, which included a million South Asians and half a million people from the Caribbean. There was in addition a 'mixed' population gain of a quarter of a million.

Halsey (1988, p.15) further notes that the influx of immigrants from the so-called 'new commonwealth' resulted in a political backlash which led to a restrictive definition of British citizenship via the Immigration Acts of 1962-71. Moreover, although some legislative attempts have been made to combat racial and ethnic discrimination, social division remains. Black people in Britain experience disadvantage and deprivation through racism and discrimination that permeates many areas of life. They are more likely than white people to be unemployed or low paid; their housing is likely to be overcrowded and lacking amenities; access to public services, even access to schools in some areas, is more difficult for them. Infant mortality is much higher in certain ethnic groups than in the rest of the population and ethnic groups have their own special health problems such as sicklecell anaemia and thalassaemia (Bradshaw, 1990, p. 40).

In 1986, ethnic minorities represented 8.1 per cent of the population aged 1-15. Indian, Pakistani and Caribbean are the largest ethnic groups, comprising over half of the total. Afro-Caribbean children and those of mixed race parentage are more likely to be admitted to local authority care than are white or Asian children. Black children are also required to make additional adjustments whilst growing up in managing the transition from or maintaining their ethnic culture (Bradshaw, 1990, p. 40). This issue has figured prominently in the recent debate about transracial adoption and fostering (Ahmed, Cheetham and Small, 1986).

A second major factor in household diversity is the increasing number of one-parent families in Britain. This has prompted concern about the future of the family; and, indeed, society's future. In Britain, divorces and the number of one-parent families have more than doubled since 1971. By 1991, Britain had the second highest divorce rate in Europe: one in three marriages. One-parent families presently comprise some 19 per cent of all families; around 28 per cent of births now take place outside marriage; and, each year, the parents of an estimated 150,000 additional children under 16 are divorced (Dennis and Erdos, 1992).

Commentators on both the left and right of the political spectrum see the family as the 'foundation stone of a free society', as the place where ...'children learn the voluntary restraint, respect for others and sense of personal responsibility without which freedom is impossible' (Dennis and Erdos, 1992)...On this view, the decline of the 'traditional family' has resulted in increased levels of crime, violence and degradation (Davies, Berger and Carlson, 1993). As previously noted, the term 'underclass' is used by Murray (1990) to refer to groups who are regarded as living outside the norms of social life, whose family ties tend to be severed, who rely on welfare benefits rather than work, and resort to crime and drugs. However, although sharing Murray's concerns, Dennis and Erdos (1992) do not accept that what they define as the problems of growing illegitimacy and family breakdown, the reduction in the work ethic and rising crime can be understood in terms of a self-contained inner-city underclass; rather, Dennis and Erdos argue that these things are signs of a general malaise in British culture.

Interestingly, Dennis writes from the standpoint of a socialist who is concerned about what he sees as a decline of socialist morality. Other attacks on single parents have come from the right. Following Murray (1990), the present administration has condemned illegitimacy and resurrected the canard of the 'deserving' and 'undeserving' poor from the last century (Durham, 1993). But critics of the Government accuse it of trying to shift the blame for increasing poverty away from social and economic policy on to the poor themselves.

Other commentators have observed that the threat of unemployment and a lack of job security have exacerbated the pressures on families over the last decade or so. In some 60 per cent of families, both parents now go out to work - often to maintain acceptable living standards. However, child-care and parental leave facilities for many working parents fall far short of what is required. In 1991, local authorities provided day care facilities for just under one per cent of children under five, and statutory maternity leave remains at just 18 weeks. Thus, many parents are obliged to make their own child-care arrangements. These are often patchy, piecemeal, and subject to breakdown (Doughty, 1994).

Critical issues and dilemmas

The increasing pressure on families has, in turn, increased the demands placed on local authority social services departments. However, rather than increasing the capacity of social welfare practitioners to meet these demands, it would appear that central government policy has had the opposite effect. The present trend towards reducing the role of the state in welfare provision has contributed to a profound contradiction which social services staff are understandably finding it difficult to resolve. The 1980s saw major changes in social policy in Britain which together amount to the most fundamental re-evaluation of welfare provision since the 1940s. Johnson (1990, p.4) relates:

> After the war a mixed economy of welfare emerged in which the state predominated with smaller roles allotted to the voluntary and commercial sectors and in which domiciliary care was left largely to families. A broad consensus concurred with the balance struck between the statutory, voluntary, commercial and informal sectors. Mrs. Thatcher and her colleagues sought to overturn these arrangements by reducing the role of the state...

It may be argued that the role of the state, as perceived by service providers, plays a major part in determining the operational definitions of such concepts as 'promoting the welfare of children in need'. Local authority SSDs represent the state. Is it now their function to continue to play a reduced role, perhaps focusing on facilitating the provision of services by the voluntary and commercial sectors? This question assumes a particular importance in light of the fact that the current political thrust is towards the community care purchasing/care manager model which encourages the targeting of services towards individuals. Alternatively, are SSDs themselves supposed to be the primary providers? If they are supposed to provide - as of course they are, if only by funding others - what level of provision is politically expected? Is it a low level, in tune with current residualist policies, or is it the all-embracing level implied by the wide definition of need contained in the Act?

It is plain that local authority Social Services Departments in England and Wales are faced with a profound dilemma. On the one hand, there is the Children Act 1989, which is widely seen as the most progressive reform of child care law this century. On the other hand, there are flourishing social policies, both inside and outside the child care field, which would seem to blatantly contradict the spirit of this reform. Hardiker (1991a, p.356) comments that "the language of 'needs' contained in the 1989 Act, is usually associated with a collectivist model of welfare, and... sits oddly in our new residualist era." Likewise Packman and Jordan (1991, p.315) note that '...concepts...like sharing responsibility between parents and the state, reaching agreements and partnerships...have a surprisingly communitarian or even collectivist ring about them...'

The conflict is perhaps most tellingly reflected in the area of resources. If a wider definition of need is to be translated into increased service provision, then obviously additional resources will be required. However, resource constraints were much in evidence in the 1980s and the situation does not appear to have changed. Johnson (1990) observed that, at the time of writing, the resources of SSDs were stretched to breaking point owing to a growth in child abuse referrals, the rise in unemployment since 1979, the increasing level of crime, policies of deinstitutionalisation, and demographic factors (Johnson, 1990, pp.183-184). He reports that:

> Over the period from 1980/81 to 1984/85 net expenditure...on the personal social services increased by 2 percent less than was required to meet increased demand, and gross expenditure increased by 3 percent less than was required. Between 1980/81 and 1985/86 almost two-thirds of local authorities fell short of the target increases of 2 percent a year, and the most recent expenditure plans indicate that between 1988/89 and 1990/91 real expenditure on the personal social services will fall by 0.7 percent...(Johnson, 1990, p.184).

There is clear evidence that resource constraints are adversely affecting the quality of services for children and their families. For example, Johnson (1990, p.184) reports that in London alone an estimated 600 children at risk are unsupervised as a consequence of staff shortages.

Our research serves to reinforce the view that the 'collectivist' philosophy manifested in the Children Act cannot be easily put into practice in an increasingly 'residualist' social policy context. There is an inherent conflict between present resource constraints and the additional resources that are required if a wider definition of need is to be reflected in increased service provision. It is worth highlighting some of the issues and conflicts encountered by local authorities in implementing the Part III of the Children Act, which directly result from this contradiction.

First, it appears that social services departments have been generally reluctant to provide guidance to social workers on the practical interpretation of such terms as 'reasonable' and 'significant'. This is possibly because they are aware that Section 17 imposes a political rather than a legal duty upon them and they are not sure what this duty is. The result is that members of the same community, and even the same family, receive different kinds and levels of service, leading to dissension in the social network of the children being served. It may be argued that social services departments have essentially three choices. First, they can allow the situation to continue as it presently exists. This is doubtless the safest choice from a political standpoint since they will not then involve themselves in the kind of controversy that has raged for so many years around the issue of poverty (see, for example, Townsend, 1979; Oppenheim,

1990). Second, they might issue guidance to social workers to the effect that children being served must not receive goods or opportunities which would normally be denied to other children in the community. Furore would doubtless result since such a policy would amount to an official endorsement of continued disadvantage for children from troubled environments. Third, they might encourage all social workers serving a particular community to decide among themselves what levels of service are appropriate in commonly-encountered situations, adding the proviso that the *family* should be served and not only the child. A decision to provide a higher level of service to all would naturally have resource implications. A decision, in the name of equality, to deprive some children of services presently being offered would inevitably provoke dissension.

A second major issue is the indication that the potential of the Act to shift the balance of service from protection to prevention is not being realised: and, indeed, the balance may even be moving in the opposite direction. Children who have already been identified as in need of services are stringently prioritised, with top priority necessarily being afforded to those suffering abuse or neglect. New obligations imposed by the Act often mean that the same amount of work takes more time, with the result that the need for prioritisation becomes greater yet, and even less is left for those at the bottom of the list than was the case before the Act. For example, no-one would deny that working in partnership with both service users and other agencies is a vital component of adequate service. However, it is also hard to deny that partnership endeavours are often costly and always time-consuming. Managing difficult meetings, containing warring parents and maintaining a balance between children's, parents' and social workers' views themselves consume a considerable proportion of scarce resources and may mean, in the long run, that better service is provided to fewer people.

Given the difficulties associated with serving children already identified, it is hardly surprising that social services departments have been slow to identify an additional population, whose needs -both present and potential - they are unlikely to be able to meet. Of course, it may be argued that identification is useful in itself since it will enable shortfalls in funding to be estimated and may uncover serious cases of actual or potential risk. Nevertheless, motivation is lacking, and the same may justifiably be said of method. Children in need, as defined in the Act, comprise a broader population than before and therefore cannot be identified merely by collation of existing data. New needs assessments are required, involving a formidable amount of work for which local social service departments do not appear to have the time, the funds, or possibly the skills.

Skills in themselves comprise another issue, particularly research skills and the relational and managerial skills required to work in partnership with other agencies. Competence in research methods is increasingly important, not only with respect to needs assessments but also in relation to monitoring and evaluation. More relevant data will be gathered in the long run, and the probability of utilisation will be higher, if social service departments themselves are able to undertake these kinds of research tasks. Inevitably, there will be resource implications since a 'skill' by definition is an expertness that comes from training, and training naturally requires funds. However, it is not just training which permits the acquisition of skills but also perceptions about the kinds of skills that may be needed. What kinds and degrees of skill should be expected from a person who is going to make a career out of serving other people? Should such a person be expected to evaluate his or her own work, keep abreast of current research, and contribute to the gaining of new knowledge? If no, then what skills are required? If yes, is the average level of attainment seen at present adequate? And if no, what might be done to improve it?

It may be argued that social workers are already expected to keep abreast of current issues, including research findings, but do not have the time to do so. Whilst case loads remain high and cases go unallocated, is it reasonable to suggest that social workers should spend time reading when they could be serving clients? A balanced answer will involve consideration of many factors, but in essence it is a matter of priorities. To what degree should quality be sacrificed for quantity? How important is it that social workers should understand and practice the basic research methods that will allow them to evaluate their work with clients? Does it matter that this type of practice is increasingly required of social workers in other countries, particularly in Canada and the United States, but it is rarely required in Britain? In the long term, it may be a matter of reviewing the skills required, in co-operation with educational institutions, and adjusting employment criteria to reflect these skills.

Skills are also at issue with respect to establishing joint protocol with other agencies for identifying children in need. Establishing inter-agency protocols for any reason is a process fraught with difficulty. Jealousies concerning territory, the perceived status of various disciplines in the professional hierarchy, conflicting structures, traditions, objectives, values, powers and duties, and the persistence of stereotypes are only a few of the problems which beset the most well-intentioned attempts to establish communication channels between agencies. Almost twenty years ago, Webb (1975) wrote:

> Better co-ordination and teamwork are a perennial desire of planners, administrators, teachers and researchers in the social services. It is

unfortunate that in Britain we have hardly begun to analyse what it is we are urging on practitioners; why it is we are doing so; how much we think it is worth paying for better co-ordination, or how we might recognise good co-ordination - or teamwork - when we see it.

The questions raised by Webb still remain to be answered from a theoretical research perspective. In the absence of a guiding framework, social service administrators themselves must answer the questions on an ad hoc basis. What specific objectives do protocols hope to achieve? How will success be measured? How much autonomy will have to be surrendered, and are departments prepared - and even permitted - to relinquish control in certain areas? Above all, what are the prevailing attitudes of social service staff towards co-operative work with other agencies? Is education needed to acquaint staff with the problems and aspirations of professionals from other disciplines?

Another factor adding to the difficulty of identifying children in need may be the reluctance of some families to be identified. Since services are inherently stigmatising in the present residualist context, despite the best efforts of social service departments to reduce the perception of stigma, it may be anticipated that some potential users will be reluctant to come forward. Data indicate that this may be the case with respect to parents of disabled children.

Stigma and privilege - opposite sides of the same coin - both have to do with receiving services denied to other society members. It follows that the fewer the number of recipients, the more prestigious or stigmatising receiving the service becomes. It is questionable whether providing service to greater numbers represents a real option in the current economic climate and, in any case, this would do nothing to solve the underlying problem. Many existing and potential service users do not want to be served and may not have to be served if they had employment income sufficient to supply their needs. The provision of non-stigmatising services cannot be achieved by local social services departments alone, or indeed by anything short of a comprehensive national strategy involving employment, housing, wages, taxation and social security policies at the very least.

None of this absolves social service departments from their immediate duty to try to reduce the perception of stigma, particularly where it is associated with poor parenting skills. Few parents with adolescent children have travelled the turbulent waters entirely unscathed. Community parent support groups are less an admission of failure than a method of self-defence; and as such they are in an excellent position to provide non-stigmatising assistance to all parents, whether served by social services departments or not. Reduction of stigma through liaison with community groups may prove to be one way in which local authorities can 'facilitate the provision by others of services...' as required by Section 17, paragraph 5.

Reduction of the perception of stigma may also be achieved to some degree by efforts to establish a genuine partnership between parents and local authorities. Part III of the Act redefines the general powers and duties of local authorities in relation to children, on the principle that parents and local authorities should work together in 'voluntary partnership' for the benefit of the children concerned (White, Carr and Lowe, 1990). However, the Act also replaces 'parental rights' with 'parental responsibility', and 'partnership' in the context of the Act therefore has much to do with support to parents in their exercise of parental responsibility. Our research indicates that an increased emphasis on parental contact and involvement means that some parents are being inappropriately urged to accept responsibility for behaviourally disturbed children whom they cannot control and of whom they are physically afraid. The Act's new emphasis on parental responsibility should not mean an abrogation of social services' own responsibility. The purpose of the Act is to find a balance between children and parents, the state and families, the courts and local authorities and, where power is unequal, to safeguard the weak. It cannot be assumed that it is always the children who are weak.

Given the quite profound contradiction between the requirements of Part III of the Act and current socio-economic and political realities, it is not surprising that local authorities are struggling with the very difficult task of fulfilling their new duties and accommodating new perspectives. Further, it should not be forgotten that the Children Act does represent a 'quantum leap from the old restricted notions of prevention to a more positive outreaching duty of support for children and families' (Packman and Jordan, 1991, p.323). Strides of similar magnitude are now required to ensure that local authorities have the capacity to fulfil their mandate.

However, we do not wish to imply that all the problems highlighted can be solved by additional resources. Formal and informal policies concerning need, together with associated activities, are determined largely by the interplay between resources, skills and attitudes. Given limited resources, it is inevitable that difficult choices will have to be made with respect to defining and prioritising the different types and levels of need. The decisions finally reached will not only reflect the current fiscal climate; they will also be influenced by the skills and attitudes of service providers. It may be argued that resources, attitudes and skills are inter-related factors. New skills, for example, can only be achieved through training, for which resources are needed; and existing skills may only be fully demonstrated if service providers are genuinely committed both to the kinds of services they are required to offer and to the people whose needs they are supposed to meet. In other words, operationalisation of the

Children Act will be affected not just by the content of the Act, nor by the resources required for its implementation, but by its entire economic, political and social context.

SUMMARY

Key points

A positive view of prevention entails the promotion of policies and practices aimed at preventing children from failing to enjoy in their own homes, the kind of parenting, the freedom from suffering, the standards of living, and the quality of community life which is considered reasonable for children in our society.

That we are far from achieving such policies and practices owes much to the fact that the basic contextual requirements for an effective system of family support are lacking. First, services are not generally decentralised on a local neighbourhood basis, and family centres have so far not been given the pivotal role in the activities of local authorities that effective family support services necessitate.

Moreover, rather than being a society that is moving towards a reduction of inequality, Britain has moved in the opposite direction over the past decade or so. Social polarisation has occurred, there is debate about the possible emergence of a distinct underclass, and levels of child poverty have increased. Additional demands have also been placed on social welfare practitioners and agencies as a result of factors associated with increasing household diversity.

Thus, we see that the Children Act has significantly enlarged the responsibilities of social welfare practitioners in relation to family support work precisely at a time when the pressures on families, particularly the most vulnerable families, have been acute.

These pressures have been exacerbated by the residual social policies of central government, which have simultaneously eroded the capacity of social welfare practitioners and agencies to offer effective support to children in need and their families.

In this chapter we have seen that many of the key issues and dilemmas confronting social welfare practitioners and agencies in operationalising need, directly result from the contradiction between the all-embracing spirit of the Act and the current political and social realities.

Perhaps more than any other factor, poverty threatens the practical achievement of effective family support services. Yet, for both policy makers and practitioners, poverty appears to have been relegated to the margin of their concerns and actions. It is as if the only way of coping with the overwhelming fact of hardcore poverty - the product of increasing inequality - is to look the other way and act as though it were not happening. Whilst understandable, perhaps, this response merely leads into a cul-de-sac of inappropriate and ineffective policy and practice. The successful implementation of Part III of the Children Act, and indeed, community care policy more widely, necessitates that poverty be placed again at the centre of the policy, practice and research agenda.

This does not imply that individuals and families who live in poverty should be transformed into 'welfare' clients in order to obtain services. Nor is it to suggest that there is there is any substitute for action at the national level to tackle primary poverty, and for steps to ensure that local authorities have the resources to carry out their mandate under Part III of the Act. We have already emphasised that a comprehensive national strategy to tackle need is required. Nevertheless, it seems to us that there are three distinct strategies through which, even in these difficult times, social welfare practitioners and agencies can at least seek to make a direct impact upon the financial circumstances of their service users.

1. Policy makers and senior officers within social welfare agencies can recognise their own status as major resource holders and the impact which their own spending decisions might make upon the impoverished communities with whom their organisations have almost all their dealings. Through patterns of employment, location of offices, choices concerning purchase of goods and materials, organisations have the capacity to invest within the human, physical and social fabric of such communities. We indicated above that the organisation of service delivery appears incompatible with the concept of family support contained in Part III of the Children Act. Family support services should be decentralised on a local neighbourhood basis, and family centres should play a pivotal role in such services.

    Currently, however, it is difficult to escape the impression that local authority social services departments tend to operate in ways that are self-defeating, that seem bound to frustrate their efforts to develop effective family support services, and that appear inimical to their attempts to fashion an authentic partnership with parents, children and local communities: workers tend to be drafted in from outside the local area,

112

operations are often directed from remote headquarters, and more appears to be sucked out of deprived communities in terms of simple financial resources than is invested within them.

2.	Within social welfare organisations, a reformulation needs to take place in traditional welfare rights activities. To begin with, these strands need reaffirmation as part of mainstream work, rather than being located at the margin of organisational activity. Social workers have long been somewhat ambivalent in their attitudes towards income maximisation. At a time when the social democratic institutions of the welfare state are under wider threat, and the policies of rationing and coercion are in the ascendency, a new style of intervention in this field has to be developed. A technocratic understanding of the labyrinthine ways in which the remnants of the welfare state doles out its remaining benefits is not sufficient. Rather, a more proactive approach is required, which recognises and seeks to redress the unfairness and discriminations within the system.

3.	With regard to the wider anti-poverty strategies of local authorities, whilst the development of Credit Unions, cooperative buying schemes and Bond banks are not solutions to primary poverty, they remain capable of producing an impact upon the financial circumstances of groups in poverty. Moreover, they do this in ways which build upon the extensive systems of mutual support which remain remarkably vigorous within the most disadvantaged communities.

Bibliography

Abbott, P. (1989), 'Family Lifestyles and Structures' in Stainton Rogers, W., Hevey, D. and Ash, E. (eds), *Child Abuse and Neglect: Facing the Challenge,* The Open University, Milton Keynes.

Ahmed, S., Cheetham, J. and Small, J. (1986), *Social Work with Black Children and their Families,* Batsford, London.

Aitchison, J. and Carter, H. (1985), *The Welsh Language 1961-1981,* University of Wales Press, Cardiff.

Aldgate, J., Tunstill, J. and McBeath, G. (1992), *National Monitoring of the Children Act: Part III section 17 - the first year,* Oxford University/NCVCCO.

Audit Commission (1994), *Seen But Not Heard: Co-ordinating Community Child Health and Social Services for Children in Need,* HMSO, London.

Barclay Committee (1982), *Social Workers: Their roles and Tasks. The Barclay Report,* Bedford Square Press, London.

Barnardo's (1990), *Missing the Target,* Barkingside, London.

Becker, S. (1991), *Windows of Opportunity: Public Policy and the Poor,* Child Poverty Action Group, London.

Becker, S. and Selburn, R. (1990), *The New Poor Clients: Social Work, Poverty and the Social Fund,* Community Care/Benefits Research Unit, Wallington.

Bowlby, J. (1952), *Maternal Care and Mental Health,* World Health Organisation, Geneva.

Bradshaw, J. (1990), *Child Poverty and Deprivation in the UK,* National Children's Bureau, London.

Bradshaw, J. (1993), *Household Budgets and Living Standards,* Joseph Rowntree Report, York.

Brown, J.C. (1990), 'The Focus on Single Mothers' in Murray, C. *The Emerging British Underclass,* Institute of Economic Affairs, London.

Children Act 1989, HMSO, London.

Community Care, 12 April 1990.

Craig, G. and Glendinning, F. (1990), *The Impact of Social Security Changes,* Barnardos, London.

Davies, J., Berger, B. and Carlson, A. (1993), *The Family: Is it Just Another Lifestyle Choice?* Institute of Economic Affairs, London.

Deakin, N. (1990), 'Mr Murray's Ark' in Murray, C. *The Emerging British Underclass,* Institute of Economic Affairs, London.

Dennis, N. and Erdos, G. (1992), *Families Without Fatherhood,* Institute of Economic Affairs, London.

Department of Health (1988), *Report of the Inquiry into Child Abuse in Cleveland,* HMSO, London.

Department of Health (1988) *Protecting Children: a guide for social workers undertaking a comprehensive investigation,* HMSO, London.

Department of Health (1989), *The Care of Children, Principles and Practice in Regulations and Guidance,* HMSO, London.

Department of Health (1991), *The Children Act 1989 Guidance and Regulations; Volume 2, Family Support, Day Care and Educational Provision for Young Children,* HMSO, London.

Department of Health and Social Security (1985), *Review of Child Care Law,* HMSO, London.

Doughty, R. (1994), 'A History of Happy Families?' *The Guardian,* 11 January, 1994.

Durham, M. (1993), 'Benefits of Tory Morality', *The Observer,* 14 November, 1993.

Elliott, L. (1994), 'CBI Attack on New Poverty', *The Guardian,* 11 March, 1994.

Field, F. (1990), 'Britain's Underclass: Countering the Growth' in Murray, C., *The Emerging British Underclass,* Institute of Economic Affairs, London.

Gardner, R. and Manby, M. (1993), 'The Children Act and Family Support: A Crisis of Values', *Adoption and Fostering,* vol. 17, no. 3, Spring.

Goldstein, J. Freud, A. and Solnit, A. (1973), *Beyond the Best Interests of the Child,* Free Press, New York.

Goldstein, J. Freud, A. and Solnit, A. (1979), *Before The Best Interests of the Child,* Free Press, New York.

Halsey, A.H., (ed.), (1988), *British Social Trends Since 1900: A Guide to the Changing Structure of Britain,* Macmillan, London.

Hardiker, P., Exton, K. and Barker, M. (1991a), 'The Social Policy Contexts of Prevention in Child Care', *British Journal of Social Work,* vol. 21, no. 4, August 1991.

Hardiker, P., Exton, K. and Barker, M. (1991b), *Policies and Practices in Preventive Child Care,* Avebury, Aldershot.

Home Office, Department of Health, Department of Education and Science, and Welsh Office (1991), *Working Together Under the Children Act 1989: A Guide to Arrangements for Inter-Agency Co-operation for the Protection of Children from Abuse*, HMSO, London.

HMSO (1992), *Households below Average Income, A Statistical Analysis, 1979 - 1988/89*, Government Statistical Service, 1992, HMSO, London.

Holman, B. (1988), *Putting Families First: Prevention and Child Care*, Macmillan, London.

House of Commons (1984), *Second Report from the Social Services Committee, Session 1983-84, Children in Care*, HMSO, London.

House of Commons (1987), *The Law on Child Care and Family Services*, HMSO, London.

Johnson, N. (1990), *Restructuring the Welfare State: A Decade of Change*, Harvester-Wheatsheaf, London.

London Borough of Brent (1985), *A Child in Trust: Report on the Death of Jasmine Beckford*, London Borough of Brent, Middlesex.

London Borough of Greenwich (1987), *A Child in Mind: The Report of the Commission of Inquiry into the Circumstances Surrounding the Death of Kimberley Carlile*, London Borough of Greenwich, Greenwich.

McNeish, D. (1993), *Liquid Gold, The Cost of Water in the 90s*, Barnardos, London.

Murray, C. (1990), *The Emerging British Underclass*, Institute of Economic Affairs, London.

National Children's Home, (1993), *A Lost Generation?* NCH, London.

National Institute for Social Work (NISW) (1982), *Social Workers: Their Roles and Tasks* (the Barclay report), Bedford Square Press, London.

Oldfield, N. and Yu, C. S. (1993), *The Cost of a Child*, Child Poverty Action Group, London.

Open University (1990), *The Children Act: Putting it into Practice,* Open University Press, Milton Keynes.

Oppenheim, C. (1990), *Poverty: The Facts,* Child Poverty Action Group, London.

Oppenheim, C. (1993), *Poverty: The Facts,* Revised and Updated Edition, Child Poverty Action Group, London.

Packman, J. (1975), *The Child's Generation*, Blackwell and Robertson, London.

Packman, J. and Jordan, B. (1991), 'The Children Act: Looking Forward, Looking Back', *The British Journal of Social Work*, vol. 21 no. 4, August.

Parker, R. (ed.), (1980), *Caring for Separated Children*, Macmillan, London.

Parton, N. (1985), *The Politics of Child Abuse*, Macmillan, London.

Pinker, R. (1979), *The Idea of Welfare,* Heinemann, London.

Rapoport, R.N., Fogarty, M.P. and Rapoport, R. (eds), (1982), *Families in Britain,* Routledge and Kegan Paul, London.

Report of the Care of Children Committee, (Curtis Report) (1946), Cmnd 6922. HMSO, London.

Report of the Committee on Children and Young Persons (Ingleby Report) (1960), Cmnd 1191. HMSO, London.

Report of the Committee on Local Authority and Allied Social Services (Seebohm report) (1968), Cmnd 3703. HMSO, London.

Rowe, J. and Lambert, L. (1973), *Children Who Wait.* Association of British Adoption and Fostering Agencies, London.

Sinfield, A., Sinfield, D., Kirk, D. and Nelson, S. (1991), *Excluding Youth,* Centre for Social Welfare Research, Edinburgh.

Stainton Rogers, R. (1989), 'The Social Construction of Childhood' in Stainton Rogers, W., Hevey, D. and Ash, E. (eds), *Child Abuse and Neglect: Facing the Challenge,* The Open University, Milton Keynes.

Stewart, G. and Stewart, J. (1993), *Social Circumstances of Younger Offenders Under Supervision,* Association of Chief Officers of Probation, London.

Stewart, G., Stewart, J., Prior, A. and Peelo, M. (1989), *Surviving Poverty: Probation Work and Benefits Policy,* ACOP, Wakefield.

Townsend, P. (1979), *Poverty in the United Kingdom,* Penquin, London.

University of Leicester and Department of Health, (1991), *Children in Need and Their Families: A New Approach; A Manual for Senior Managers on Part III of the Children Act 1989,* University of Leicester.

Walker, A. (1990), 'Blaming the Victims' in Murray, C., *The Emerging British Underclass,* Institute of Economic Affairs, London.

Webb, A. (1975), 'Co-ordination between Health and Personal Social Services: A Question of Quality', Unpublished paper presented to European Seminar on Interaction of Social Welfare and Health Personnel in the Delivery of Services: Implications for Training.

White, R., Carr, P. and Lowe, N. (1990), *A Guide to the Children Act,* Butterworths, London.

Index

abuse 7, 8, 12, 15, 25-26, 76, 79,
    97, 106
    priority given to 23, 25, 37-41
    see also, sexual abuse
accommodation 13, 14, 15, 28, 40,
    41-3, 50, 51, 81
adoption 7-8, 10, 28
    and race issues 87, 90, 96, 103
    see also fostering
alcohol abuse, *see* drug/alcohol
    abuse
appropriate adult 76
assessment of need 26, 27, 91, 93,
    96, 108
    data on 26, 27
    guidance to social workers on 35,
    36
    interagency co-operation in 31
    social workers' criteria for 36, 37,
    75
Audit Commission Report 1994
    79-80, 81

Barclay Report 9, 10, 16,
Beckford Report 12
bed and breakfast accommodation
    25, 66, 81

child emigration 3, 4, 8
Children Act 1948 4, 5, 16
Children Act 1975 8, 11, 16
Children Act 1989

aims of 12-13
    context of 10-12, 16-17
    key issues in 2, 30, 33-44, 97
    origins of 3-12, 16
Children and Young Persons Act
    1952 5
Children and Young Persons Act
    1963 5
Children and Young Persons Act
    1969 6
Children Bill 1975 7-8
children in need
    affected by inadequate services
        41-2, 45
    categories of 15, 23, 25-6, 28, 33
    identification of, *see* ident-
        ification of children in need
    prioritisation of, *see* prioritisation
        of children in need
    social justice definition of 15, 98
children with disabilities 27-30
    categories of 14
    data about 28, 30, 32
    duties towards 15, 28-9, 51, 58
    integrated services 28
    joint services for 28, 30
    priority towards 38-9, 41, 45
    register of, *see* register of
        children with disabilities
    services to 28-9, 32, 46
children's information 61-2, 65, 70
children's participation

in reviews 59, 62
in decision-making 62-3, 65
views taken notice of 63, 70
children's satisfaction 65
related to unmet needs 63
relationship with social worker
63, 64, 66-7, 70-71
class 3, 4, 7, 17
see also underclass
Cleveland Report 12
complaint, definition of 65
complaints procedures 64-5
children's knowledge of 64, 71
in Children Act 1989 19, 64-5,
independent element in 64
parents' knowledge of 64, 66, 71
publication of 19, 20, 64, 66,
71-2
cost estimates, for meeting
identified needs 26, 27, 31
counselling 14, 28, 41, 42, 43, 45,
54, 57
cultural issues 86-96
addressed in Children Act 1989
13, 86, 94
ethnic needs, *see* ethnic needs
in policy documents 86-7
related to identification of need
86, 91, 93, 95
religious needs, *see* religious
needs
Welsh culture, *see* Welsh culture
Curtis Report 4

data
demographic 91, 94-5, 96
on numbers of children in various
categories of need 26, 27, 28
related to identification of
children in need 26-7, 28, 31
day care 13, 15, 28, 41, 43, 45, 46,

104
definition of need 14-16, 33
adequacy of 35-6, 37
broad definition of 23, 33, 35,
105, 106
narrow definition of 23, 35
social workers' attitudes
towards 33-4, 37
social workers' interpretation of
36-7, 38
delinquency 6, 15, 25, 38, 39, 45,
49-50, 67, 68
parents' concerns about 50, 51,
52, 54, 56
disability
Children Act 1989
definition of disability, *see*
children with disabilities
diversity
childhood 102-04, 111
ethnic 103
divorce 15, 100, 103-04
drug/alcohol abuse 49, 50, 52, 54,
55, 56, 61, 63, 64, 68, 69, 71,
78, 100, 104
rehabilitation 67, 69

emotional abuse, *see* abuse
ethnic needs 2, 13, 37, 42, 86
data on 91, 95
difficulties in meeting 42
reference to in policy documents
86-7
ethnic monitoring 91, 92, 93, 96

family centres 15, 41, 42, 43, 45,
46, 49, 58, 72, 98-99, 111, 112
family support 1, 2, 12, 13, 16, 17,
98
conditions required for 98-100,
111, 112

joint protocols with statutory
agencies 58-9, 76, 78-9, 81, 82,
84, 85, 109
nature of 58, 78
related to identification of
children in need 108
joint protocols with voluntary
agencies 76

labelling 50, 68, 74, 75
see also stigma
learning disability, *see* disability
leaving care 38, 39, 60, 63, 71, 75,
80, 81
priority given to 42, 45-6
local authority care, see
accommodation
linguistic needs, *see* cultural issues

monitoring
necessity for 77, 83
of policies 19
procedures for 20, 24, 30, 31, 83,
108

National Assistance Act 1948 5
National Childrens Home 3
neglect 5, 15, 25, 26, 37, 38, 39,
40, 45, 48, 49, 68, 70, 97, 107

parental responsibility 12, 14, 47,
51, 57, 68, 110
parents' information
on available services 54, 55, 58,
59-60
on complaints procedures 64, 65
parents' participation
with regard to children being
accommodated 55, 58, 63
in reviews 55, 58
in decision making 55, 58

views taken notice of 70
parents' satisfaction
related to help in bringing up
children 50
related to unmet needs 43, 54, 57
with services provided 50-51, 52
partnership with children
61-2, 63, 65-6, 72, 112
partnership with parents 12, 18, 47,
51, 52, 61, 66, 68, 69, 72, 112
physical abuse *see* abuse
polarisation 99-100, 111
police 2, 57, 67, 68, 71, 73, 75, 76,
78, 79, 81, 83, 84, 90
policies
multicultural 89, 90, 91, 92, 93,
96
unwritten 20, 89, 94
policy documents 18, 30, 77-8,
86
monitoring of 19, 30
writing goals into 18-24, 30-31
Poor Law 2-3, 4, 100
Poor Law Amendment Act 1834 3
poverty 5, 7, 8, 15, 16, 25, 39, 40,
45, 46, 68, 71, 75, 100, 101-02,
104, 111, 112-14
preventive services 10, 16, 52, 69
see also family support services
prevention 2-10, 11, 12, 15, 16, 23,
27, 89, 110, 111
meaning of 97-8
model of 40-41
prevention vs protection 27, 32,
36-8, 44-5, 107
prioritising levels of 40-41, 43
social workers' views on 39
prioritisation of 'children in need'
25, 38-41
proactive preventive services 36,
38, 40, 44, 95, 99, 113

children with disabilities 29, 30,
  32
related to service provision 3, 4,
  14, 16, 89, 95, 109
related to voluntary agency
  participation 4, 109-10

teenage pregnancy 43, 52, 56, 57,
  59
training 35, 82, 92-3, 108, 110
  child protection 8
  joint training 38, 45, 85, 88, 96
  race awareness 92, 93
  relevancy of 93, 95-6
  in Welsh language 93, 96
truancy 49, 56, 68, 74, 78, 100
  parents' concerns about 49-50, 52,
  54, 57, 78

unemployment 99-100, 101, 103,
  104, 105

underclass 100-101, 104, 111
unmet needs
  childrens' 43, 57, 63
  parents' 43, 54, 57

voluntary organisations 27, 42, 73,
  105
  establishment of 2, 3-4
  interagency co-operation with 27,
    28, 31, 38, 44, 69, 76-7, 82-4
  services publicised 60

welfare 3, 4, 6, 16, 72, 99, 104-5,
  112
Welsh culture and language 88-90
  policies on 89
  related to service provision 89,
    90
  training in 93